The Simple Truth Workbook

Written by Aaron Erhardt

Questions by Andy Sochor

ERHARDT PUBLICATIONS

The Simple Truth Workbook
Copyright © 2014

All Rights Reserved. No portion of this book may be reproduced in any form without the written permission of the publisher, except in the case of brief excerpts to be used in a review.

Published by:
Erhardt Publications
Louisville, Kentucky
www.ErhardtPublications.com

Printed in the United States of America

ISBN: 978-0-9860412-8-0

Table of Contents

Plan of Salvation (Part 1)	1
Plan of Salvation (Part 2)	9
Plan of Salvation (Part 3)	19
Work of the Church	27
Worship of the Church (Part 1)	37
Worship of the Church (Part 2)	47
Organization of the Church	57
Denominationalism	69
Falling From Grace	75
Wearing Religious Titles	81
The Kingdom	85
Quick Tips for Study	91
Conclusion	95

Lesson 1

Plan of Salvation (Part 1)

The most important question that a person could ask is, "What must I do to be saved?" The answer to that question is clearly revealed in the New Testament.

God wants all men to be saved. Paul wrote, "God…will have all men to be saved, and to come unto the knowledge of the truth" (1 Tim. 2:3-4). Peter added, "The Lord is not slack concerning his promise, as some men count slackness; but is longsuffering to us-ward, not willing that any should perish, but that all should come to repentance" (2 Pet. 3:9). The invitation is open and available to every person who will accept it. That is why Jesus commissioned His disciples to go "into all the world" and preach the gospel to "every creature" (Mk. 16:15).

God's love is too great to describe with words. He sent His only begotten Son to die for the sins of the world. Can you even imagine that? What earthly father do you know that would send his son to die for the mistakes and transgressions of others? I know of none. Yet God did just that! John wrote, "In this was manifested the love of God toward us, because that God sent his only begotten Son into the world, that we might live through him. Herein is love, not that we loved God, but that he loved us, and sent his Son to be the propitiation for our sins…And we have seen and do testify that the Father sent the Son to be the Savior of the world" (1 Jn. 4:9-10, 14). Notice that God sent Jesus (1) that we might live through Him, (2) to be the propitiation for our sins, and (3) to be the Savior of the world. He loved us that much. Consider the passage below.

> John 3:16 — "For God (greatest person) so loved (greatest motive) the world, that he gave his only begotten Son (greatest gift), that whosoever (greatest invitation) believeth in him should not perish, but have everlasting life (greatest promise)."

One must also stand in awe of the Lord's love for mankind. In harmony with the Father's will, He voluntarily left the glories of heaven to die on the cross. He did not have to come; He chose to come. He did for us what we could not have done for ourselves. He brought hope to the hopeless and life to the lifeless. "The Son of Man came not to be ministered unto, but to minister, and give his life a ransom for many" (Matt. 20:28). "For the Son of Man is come to seek and to save that which is lost" (Lk. 19:10). "Christ hath redeemed us from the curse of the law, being made a curse for us" (Gal. 3:13). "Christ Jesus came into the world to save sinners" (1 Tim. 1:15). "Who gave himself for us, that he might redeem us from all iniquity" (Tit. 2:14). "Who his own self bare our sins in his own body on the tree, that we, being dead to sins, should live unto righteousness" (1 Pet. 2:24). "For Christ also hath once suffered for sins, the just for the unjust, that he might bring us to God" (1 Pet. 3:18). He loved us that much.

> "Jesus Christ, moved by a love, a compassion, tenderer and stronger than human hearts can ever know, shared man's weaknesses, his sorrows, his sufferings, his shame, his death, that he might thereby lift man out of his degradation, his sin, his ruin, to share with him life and joy from the throne of God forever" (*Salvation From Sin*, David Lipscomb, p. 68).

Calvinists erroneously teach that God predestined some individuals to be lost before the foundation of the world, and there is nothing they can do to change their fate. However, the Bible says that Christ "died for all" (2 Cor. 5:14), "tasted death for every man" (Heb. 2:9), and is "the propitiation...for the sins of the whole world" (1 Jn. 2:2). Hence, all men have the opportunity to be saved. In fact, if Calvinism were true, God would be a respecter of persons, which He is not (Acts 10:34). It would also make God responsible for man being lost, which He is not (2 Cor. 5:10). Who can believe such nonsense? The Bible is filled with passages indicating that man has a choice in his salvation. "Choose you this day whom ye will serve" (Josh. 24:15). "Come unto me, all ye that labor and are heavy laden, and I will give you rest" (Matt. 11:28). "Save yourselves from this untoward generation" (Acts 2:40). "Work out your own salvation with fear and trembling" (Phil. 2:12). Why would all these passages, and a host of others, be in the Bible if man was already predestined, and there was nothing he could do to change his fate? Furthermore, why would Jesus say of the unbelieving Jews, "Ye will not come to me" (Jn. 5:40)? If Calvinism were true, shouldn't He have said, "Ye can not come to me?" The same is true about the comments Jesus made when lamenting about Jerusalem. He said, "Ye would not" come to me, not "ye could not" come to me. Obviously Calvinism is a false doctrine. God predestined the plan, not the man.

Consider this: If sinners have no capacity to believe, why did Jesus marvel at unbelief (Mark 6:6)?

Barton W. Stone, a prominent member of the restoration movement, preached Calvinistic doctrine in the Presbyterian Church before learning the truth. He recalled, "Often when I was addressing the listening multitudes on the doctrine of total depravity, their inability to believe — and of the necessity of the physical power of God to produce faith; and then persuading the helpless to repent and believe the gospel, my zeal in a moment would be chilled at the contradiction. How can they believe? How can they repent? How can they do impossibilities? How can they be guilty in not doing them? Such thoughts would almost stifle utterance, and were as mountains pressing me down to the shades of death...From this state of perplexity I was relieved by the precious Word of God. From reading and meditating upon it, I became convinced that God did love the whole world, and that the reason why he did not save all, was because of their unbelief; and that the reason why they believed not, was not because God did not exert his physical, almighty power in them to make them believe, but because they neglected and received not his testimony, given in the Word concerning his Son" (*The Cane Ridge Reader*, Barton W. Stone, pp. 32-33). Amen.

The Exclusive Savior

While the gospel is available to all men, the plan itself is very exclusive in nature. Jesus Christ is the one and only way to heaven. He declared, "If ye believe not that I am he, ye shall die in your sins" (Jn. 8:24) and "I am the way, the truth, and the life: no man cometh to the Father, but by me" (Jn. 14:6). Peter added, "Neither is there salvation in any other: for there is none other name under heaven given among men, whereby we must be saved" (Acts 4:12). Although it is not politically correct to say that nowadays, it is most certainly true. No Jew, Muslim, Hindu, Buddhist, or atheist has the hope of eternal life because they reject Jesus as the Christ. The Bible says, "And this is the record, that God hath given us eternal life, and this life is in his Son" (1 Jn. 5:11). Salvation is found in Jesus Christ alone.

Grace

Grace is unmerited favor or undeserved blessing. We are saved by the grace of God (2 Tim. 1:9; Tit. 2:11). There is nothing that man can do to earn his salvation from sin. It is a gift. Paul wrote, "For by grace are ye saved through faith; and that not of yourselves: it is the gift of God" (Eph. 2:8). Grace, however, is conditioned upon man's obedient faith. For instance, Noah was saved from the flood by grace (Gen. 6:8). Yet he had to build an ark. Would any argue that by building the ark Noah somehow earned his salvation? No. We all recognize that his obedient faith did not earn his salvation. It was simply the conditions of the grace (Heb. 11:7). Consider some other examples.

By Grace	Condition
Israelites healed of snakebite	Look on serpent of brass (Num. 21)
Israelites conquered Jericho	March around walls (Josh. 6)
Naaman healed of leprosy	Dip in Jordan River (2 Kgs. 5)
Ten lepers healed	Show the priests (Lk. 17)
Blind man given sight	Wash in pool of Siloam (Jn. 9)
Men saved from drowning	Abide in the ship (Acts 27)
Jews sins remitted	**Repent and be baptized (Acts 2)**

If grace were appropriated unconditionally as some say, then every person on earth would be saved. Think about it. Every murderer, rapist, whoremonger, blasphemer, idolater, liar, and adulterer would be heaven-bound. Yet we know that such is not the case. Jesus said, "Enter ye in at the strait gait: for wide is the gate, and broad is the way, that leadeth to destruction, and many there be which go in thereat: Because strait is the gait, and narrow is the way, which leadeth unto life, and few there be that find it" (Matt. 7:13-14). God's grace is conditioned upon man's obedient faith.

Steps of Salvation

(1) **Hear.** The road to salvation starts with hearing the gospel of Jesus Christ. "So then faith cometh by hearing, and hearing by the word of God" (Rom. 10:17). The book of Acts clearly indicates that the one being converted to Christ heard the gospel preached before he believed and obeyed (4:4; 18:8).

(2) **Believe.** A person must believe the gospel of Jesus Christ. "I said therefore unto you, that ye shall die in your sins: for if ye believe not that I am he, ye shall die in your sins" (Jn. 8:24). "But without faith it is impossible to please him: for he that cometh to God must believe that he is, and that he is a rewarder of them that diligently seek him" (Heb. 11:6).

While we are justified by faith (Rom. 5:1), we are not justified by faith only. If that were the case, we would be justified without grace (Rom. 3:24) and the blood (Rom. 5:9). Surely no one believes that. Then it is not by faith only. In fact, did you know that the only time the words "by faith only" appear in scripture, there is a not before it? It's true. James wrote, "Ye see then how that by works a man is justified, and not by faith only" (Jam. 2:24). Furthermore, if a person is justified by faith only, how do you explain the chief rulers of John 12? The Bible says, "Nevertheless among the chief rulers also many believed on him; but because of the Pharisees they did not confess him, lest they should be put out of the synagogue: For they loved the praise of men more than the praise of God" (vv. 42-43). Notice that they "believed on him." Does that mean they were justified in the sight of God? No. Then it takes more than just mere faith! The scriptures teach that in order to be saved man must obey the truth (Gal. 3:1), strive to enter (Lk. 13:24), work righteousness (Acts 10:35), do the will of the Father (Matt. 7:21), walk in the light (1 Jn. 1:7), abide in the doctrine (2 Jn. 9), and keep His commandments (Rev. 22:14).

(3) **Repent.** A person must repent of his sins. "I tell you, Nay: but, except ye repent, ye shall all likewise perish" (Lk. 13:3). "And the times of this ignorance God winked at; but now commandeth all men everywhere to repent" (Acts 17:30).

Some argue that repentance comes before faith. Not so. Faith is what leads one to repentance. For instance, the people of Nineveh heard the preaching of Jonah, believed it, and then repented of their wickedness. The Bible says, "And Jonah began to enter into the city a day's journey, and he cried, and said, Yet forty days, and Nineveh shall be overthrown. So the people of Nineveh believed God, (faith) and proclaimed a fast, and put on sackcloth, from the greatest of them even to the least of them. For word came unto the king of Nineveh, and he arose from his throne, and he laid his robe from him, and covered him with sackcloth, and sat in ashes. And he caused it to be proclaimed and published through Nineveh, by the decree of the king and his nobles, saying, Let neither man nor beast, herd nor flock, taste any thing; let them not feed, nor drink water; But let man and beast be covered with sackcloth, and cry mightily unto God; yea, let them turn every one from his evil way, and from the violence that is in their hands (repentance). Who can tell if God will turn and repent, and turn away from his fierce anger, that we perish not? And God saw their works, that they turned from their evil way; and God repented of the evil, that he had said that he would do unto them; and did it not" (Jon. 3:4-10). Notice that they first believed and then repented. Furthermore, the Jews on Pentecost heard the preaching of Peter, believed it, and then repented and were baptized (Acts 2:14-41). Hence, faith is what leads one to repentance.

Repentance is a change of one's mind that results in a change of life. An excellent example of what it truly means to repent can be seen in the parable of the two sons. Jesus said, "But what think ye? A certain man had two sons; and he came to the first, and said, Son, go work today in my vineyard. He answered and said, I will not; but afterward he repented, and went. And he came to the second, and said likewise. And he answered and said, I go, sir: and went not. Whether of them twain did the will of his father? They say unto him, the first. Jesus saith unto them, Verily I say unto you, That the publicans and the harlots go into the kingdom of God before you" (Matt. 21:28-31). Notice that in the parable the man told each of his sons to go work in the vineyard. One said he would, but never did. The other said he would not, "but afterward he repented, and went." That is exactly what it means to repent. It is a change of one's mind that results in a change of life.

A display of repentance took place during Paul's third missionary journey. When he preached the gospel to the people of Ephesus, we read, "And many that believed came, and confessed, and showed their deeds. Many of them also which used curious arts brought their books together, and burned them before all men: and they counted the price of them, and found it fifty thousand pieces of silver" (Acts 19:18-19). Notice that these new believers burned their books of sorcery and witchcraft in a public display of repentance. Their change of mind resulted in a change of life. By the way, the books they destroyed valued at over one million dollars by current standards!

Instead of using the word "repent" as most versions do, the New Century Version (NCV) says: "Change your hearts and lives." That rendering is precisely the idea being expressed. When one repents, he changes his heart and life. Without that change, there is no repentance.

(4) **Confess.** A person must confess his faith publicly. "Whosoever therefore shall confess me before men, him will I confess also before my Father which is in heaven" (Matt. 10:32). "For with the heart man believeth unto righteousness; and with the mouth confession is made unto salvation" (Rom. 10:10).

There seems to be some confusion or misunderstanding as to what we are to confess. The conversion account of the eunuch may help to clear up the confusion. The Bible says, "Then Philip opened his mouth, and began at the same scripture, and preached unto him Jesus. And as they went on their way, they came unto a certain water: and the eunuch said, See, here is water; what doth hinder me to be baptized? And Philip said, If thou believest with all thine heart, thou mayest. And he answered and said, I believe that Jesus Christ is the Son of God. And he commanded the chariot to stand still: and they went down both into the water, both Philip and the eunuch; and he baptized him" (Acts 8:35-38). Notice that the eunuch confessed his faith in Jesus Christ as the Son of God. This is the proper confession to be made before men.

Timothy, the young evangelist, made the same good confession of faith before many witnesses (1 Tim. 6:12). We know that it was the same confession because it is likened unto the confession Jesus made before Pilate (1 Tim. 6:13). What had Jesus confessed? He had confessed that He was the Son of God (Matt. 27:39-43).

(5) **Be Baptized.** A person must be baptized in water. "He that believeth and is baptized shall be saved; but he that believeth not shall be damned" (Mk. 16:16). "Then Peter said unto them, Repent, and be baptized every one of you in the name of Jesus Christ for the remission of sins, and ye shall receive the gift of the Holy Ghost" (Acts 2:38).

Baptism stands between a sinner and his salvation (Mk. 16:16), a sinner and the remission of sins (Acts 2:38), a sinner and the washing away of sins (Acts 22:16), a sinner and the death of Christ (Rom. 6:3), a sinner and the body of Christ (1 Cor. 12:13), a sinner and putting on Christ (Gal. 3:27), and a sinner and being quickened with Christ (Col. 2:12-13). Obviously baptism is an essential part of salvation.

Consider this: If to refuse John's baptism was to "reject the counsel of God" (Lk. 7:30), what about those who refuse the Lord's baptism? Is their condition any better?

Questions on Lesson 1

1. Who does God want to be saved?

2. What do Calvinists teach about predestination? How is this different than the Bible's description of predestination?

3. In whom is salvation found?

4. Define grace.

5. What is grace conditioned upon?

6. Does grace being conditional mean that man can earn his salvation? Explain.

7. What are the steps of salvation?

8. The phrase "faith only" appears only once in the Bible (Jam. 2:24). Explain the meaning of the passage.

9. Is baptism essential for our salvation? Explain.

Lesson 2

Plan of Salvation (Part 2)

The previous lesson ended with a look at the steps of salvation. This lesson picks up there, beginning with a more detailed look at the necessity of water baptism.

Mark 16:16

Few passages have been butchered more than Mark 16:16. Men have said everything from "it is not authentic" to "Jesus misspoke" in order to avoid having to answer it. However, when this world is dissolved with fire the words of Jesus will still stand true — "He that believeth and is baptized shall be saved." There is no escaping it. Why then do so many people distort and pervert the truth about baptism? Consider the chart below.

Which is the Scriptural Pattern in Mark 16:16?
Catholicism: Baptized — Saved — Believe
Protestantism: Believe — Saved — Baptized
Jesus Christ: Believe — Baptized — Saved

Catholicism and Protestantism have the wrong pattern in Mark 16:16. The Lord taught belief then baptism then salvation. Surely you can see that to be true. The doctrinal patterns of both Catholicism and Protestantism are contrary to the divine pattern of King Jesus. Faithful churches of Christ, which are not Roman Catholic or Protestant, continue to preach the scriptural pattern as revealed in Mark 16:16: believe — baptized — saved.

Some argue that the baptism of Mark 16:16 is Holy Spirit baptism, not water baptism. We know that such is not the case, however, based on the writings of Matthew. Bible students recognize that Mark 16:15-16 and Matthew 28:19-20 are both records of the same event — The Great Commission. They are parallel accounts. Matthew tells us that this baptism is (1) administered by man, and (2) in the name of. Holy Spirit baptism is not administered by man and is not in the name of. Water baptism is. Therefore, we can confidently conclude that water baptism is the baptism of Mark 16:16.

Some dispute has occurred over Mark 16:16b. It is argued that since Jesus did not say "and is baptized not," baptism is not essential to salvation. Allow me to answer that argument in two points: (1) Suppose I said, "He that eats and digests shall live, but he that eats not shall die." Would any argue that since I did not include "and digests not" that digestion is not necessary? No. Or suppose I said, "He that enrolls and attends shall be educated, but he that does not enroll shall be ignorant." Would any argue that since I did not include "and attends not" that attending is not necessary? No. The same is true with Mark 16:16b. It was not necessary to say "and is baptized not." (2) If Jesus had said "and is baptized not," He would have left two groups of people being neither saved nor damned. Think about it. What about those who believed but were not baptized? What about those who were baptized but did not believe? Both groups would be left neither saved nor damned. Surely you see the point.

If one will put aside his preconceived ideas and prejudices he will see that Mark 16:16 is very easy to understand. An alien sinner must believe (condition 1) and be baptized (condition 2) to be saved.

Beware of Baptist "Nots"

When Satan tempted Eve in the garden, he twisted the truth by employing the little word "not." Whereas God had said they would "surely die" if they ate the forbidden fruit (Gen. 2:17), Satan said they would "not surely die" (Gen. 3:4). Do you see how cunning he was? He did not present a lengthy discourse to Eve. He simply added the word "not." Unfortunately, the Baptist Church has followed in Satan's footsteps. They also twist the truth by employing the little word "not." Consider the following passages.

> Jesus: "He that believes and is baptized shall be saved" (Mk. 16:16).
> Baptists: "He that believes and is *not* baptized shall be saved."

> Peter: "Baptism doth also now save us" (1 Pet. 3:21).
> Baptists: "Baptism doth *not* also now save us."

I challenge any Baptist preacher in the world to say that they have been misrepresented in the above statements. They can't. Baptists believe and teach that one is saved before and without baptism. Thus they add a "not" to Mark 16:16 and 1 Peter 3:21.

The Blood of Christ

Redemption is made possible by the precious blood of Jesus Christ (Matt. 26:28; Eph. 1:7; Col. 1:14). There is no other acceptable remedy for sin. It took the only begotten Son of God leaving the glories of heaven and shedding His blood on the cross for mankind to be forgiven of his sins and to be reconciled to God. Peter wrote, "Forasmuch as ye know that ye were not redeemed with corruptible things, as silver and gold, from your vain conversation received by tradition from your fathers; But with the precious blood of Christ, as of a lamb without blemish and without spot" (1 Pet. 1:18-19). The blood of Christ is redeeming (Eph. 1:7), justifying (Rom. 5:9), reconciling (Col. 1:20), sanctifying (Heb. 13:12), cleansing (1 Jn. 1:7), and nigh making (Eph. 2:13). It is truly invaluable.

Many people fail to realize when we come in contact with the saving blood of Christ. They assume it is contacted when they first believe or say a prayer asking for forgiveness. However, the scriptures reveal that we contact the blood when we are baptized. Consider the chart below.

Blood	Baptism
Remits (Matt. 26:28)	Remits (Acts 2:38)
Washes (Rev. 1:5)	Washes (Acts 22:16)
Cleanses (1 Jn. 1:7)	Cleanses (Eph. 5:26)
Saves (Rom. 5:9)	Saves (1 Pet. 3:21)

The Lord's blood was shed so that you and I could be forgiven of our sins. Approximately 700 years before the crucifixion of Christ, Isaiah wrote, "Surely he hath borne our griefs, and carried our sorrows: yet we did esteem him stricken, smitten of God, and afflicted. But he was wounded for our transgressions, and he was bruised for our iniquities; the chastisement of our peace was upon him; and with his stripes we are healed" (Is. 53:4-5). Yet the scriptures teach that we contact the blood when we are baptized.

Remission of Sins

Baptism is connected to the remission of sins. We know that to be true because Peter said, "Repent and be baptized every one of you in the name of Jesus Christ *for the remission of sins*, and ye shall receive the gift of the Holy Ghost" (Acts 2:38, emphasis mine). Notice that Peter told the Jews to be baptized "for the remission of sins." Other versions render that expression "unto the remission of sins" (ASV), "so that your sins may be forgiven" (NRSV), and "then God will forgive your sins" (ERV). Hence, baptism is connected to the remission of sins.

The Greek preposition "for" (*eis*) means in order to obtain. It looks ahead to a result. Even a Baptist scholar, Edgar J. Goodspeed, recognized that fact in his translation of Acts 2:38. It says, "In order to have your sins forgiven." That rendering is precisely the point.

The Thief

When discussing the necessity of baptism, the thief on the cross usually becomes a point of emphasis. People ask, "Wasn't the thief on the cross saved without baptism?" Allow me to answer that question in five points: (1) The thief on the cross may have been baptized by John (Matt. 3:5-6) or by the disciples of the Lord (Jn. 4:1-3). We do not know. One could just as easily assume that he was baptized, as to assume that he was not baptized. (2) The thief lived under a different covenant than we do. He lived during the Mosaic Law, before Christ shed His blood and before the baptism of Christ was commanded. (3) The will of the testator does not take effect until he dies (Heb. 9:16-17). Therefore, Jesus could forgive the thief as He pleased. Now, however, His testament, which commands baptism for the remission of sins, is in effect. (4) The thief was not an alien sinner. He, being a Jew, was already in the covenant relationship. He was simply an erring child of God. (5) The thief could not believe that God raised Christ from the dead (Rom. 10:9). Does that mean we don't have to believe it either? What proves too much proves nothing at all!

Consider this: Baptism is a command (Acts 10:48). One must "do his commandments" to be saved (Rev. 22:14). What then is the condition of those who refuse baptism?

New Testament baptism is not just some "outward sign of an inward grace" as Baptist preachers would have us to believe. It is an essential part of the plan of salvation. Consider the passages below.

Mark 16:16 — "He that believeth and is baptized shall be saved; but he that believeth not shall be damned."

John 3:5 — "Verily, verily, I say unto thee, Except a man be born of water and of the Spirit, he cannot enter into the kingdom of God."

Acts 2:38 — "Then Peter said unto them, Repent, and be baptized every one of you in the name of Jesus Christ for the remission of sins, and ye shall receive the gift of the Holy Ghost."

Acts 22:16 — "Arise, and be baptized, and wash away thy sins, calling on the name of the Lord."

Romans 6:3 — "Know ye not, that so many of us as were baptized into Jesus Christ were baptized into his death?"

1 Corinthians 12:13 — "For by one Spirit are we all baptized into one body, whether we be Jews or Gentiles, whether we be bond or free; and have been all made to drink into one Spirit."

Galatians 3:27 — "For as many of you as have been baptized into Christ have put on Christ."

Colossians 2:12 — "Buried with him in baptism, wherein also ye are risen with him through the faith of the operation of God, who hath raised him from the dead."

Titus 3:5 — "Not by works of righteousness which we have done, but according to his mercy he saved us, by the washing of regeneration, and renewing of the Holy Ghost."

Hebrews 10:22 — "Let us draw near with a true heart in full assurance of faith, having our hearts sprinkled from an evil conscience, and our bodies washed with pure water."

1 Peter 3:21 — "The like figure whereunto even baptism doth also now save us (not the putting away of the filth of the flesh, but the answer of a good conscience toward God) by the resurrection of Jesus Christ."

When Should I Be Baptized?

Baptism was an urgent matter in the first century. It was performed as soon as possible. For instance, Ananias asked Saul, "Why tarriest thou? Arise, and be baptized, and wash away thy sins, calling on the name of the Lord" (Acts 22:16). Notice the urgency in the statement by Ananias: "Why tarriest thou?" (KJV) — "Why do you delay?" (NRSV) — "Why do you wait?" (ESV) — "Why wait any longer?" (NCV) — "What are you waiting for?" (NIV). Furthermore, the thousands of Jews on Pentecost were baptized "the same day" (Acts 2:41), the eunuch was baptized in the desert "as they went on their way" (Acts 8:36), and the jailor was baptized "the same hour of the night" (Acts 16:33). Baptism is not to be delayed or postponed. It is a mistake to schedule a baptism for a later date. It should be done immediately.

Infant Baptism

The Roman Catholic Church and several other denominations practice infant baptism. They believe that infants are born in sin and need to be baptized soon after birth in order to receive forgiveness. However, the baptism of infants originated with man, not God. New Testament baptism was for those who had matured enough to hear, believe, and obey. Consider the chart below.

New Testament Baptism	Infant Baptism
Taught (Matt. 28:19)	Untaught
Believers (Mk. 16:16)	Unbelievers
Repentant (Acts 2:38)	Unrepentant
Men and Women (Acts 8:12)	Infants
Confessors (Acts 8:35-38)	Non-Confessors
Sinners (Acts 22:16)	Sinless

From the above chart we see that an infant is not a proper candidate for baptism. He cannot be taught, believe, repent, or confess. Nor is he in sin (Ezek.

18:20; Matt. 19:14). The man does not live who can find the chapter and verse for infant baptism. It is unscriptural. There is neither precept nor example of infant baptism in the New Testament.

In Acts 8, the eunuch heard the gospel and asked to be baptized. Philip responded, "*If* thou believest with all thine heart, thou mayest" (v. 37, emphasis mine). This proves again that one must believe before he is a proper candidate for baptism. In other words, baptism is conditioned upon faith.

Some argue that the "household baptisms" in the New Testament included infants. Such reasoning is based totally on assumption, without any evidence from the passages at all. In fact, the evidence shows otherwise. Let us consider some "household baptisms."

> **Cornelius.** His household feared God (Acts 10:2), heard the gospel (Acts 10:33), believed the gospel (Acts 11:17), and had their hearts purified by faith (Acts 15:9). Infants can't do that.

> **Philippian Jailor.** His household was able to comprehend the gospel (Acts 16:32) and believed in God (Acts 16:34). Infants can't do that.

> **Stephanas.** His household devoted themselves to ministering to the saints (1 Cor. 16:15). Infants can't do that.

> **Lydia.** Though we do not have a lot of detail about her household, one could only assume (1) that she was married, (2) that she had children, (3) that her children were infants, and (4) that her infant children were with her. It is more likely that her household consisted of either employees or slaves.

There is no evidence in the New Testament to support the practice of infant baptism. It is a perversion of the truth. Baptism is for those who are capable of understanding the gospel and believing in Christ for themselves.

Immersion

New Testament baptism is an immersion in water. The Greek word for "baptism" (*baptisma*) means to immerse or to plunge. It consists of the process "of immersion, submersion, and emergence" (*Vine's Complete Expository Dictionary*, p.

50). All reputable sources, without exception, give immersion as the common and primary sense of the word. There is no indication whatsoever that sprinkling or pouring was practiced in the early church. Baptism was always a burial. Paul wrote, "Therefore we are buried with him by baptism into death: that like as Christ was raised up from the dead by the glory of the Father, even so we also should walk in newness of life" (Rom. 6:4) and "Buried with him in baptism, Wherein also ye are risen up with him through the operation of God, who hath raised him from the dead" (Col. 2:12). Just as a dead body is completely buried in dirt, the subject for baptism is to be completely buried in water. Furthermore, the fact that John baptized in Aenon "because there was much water there" (Jn. 3:23) confirms that baptism was an immersion in water. Sprinkling or pouring for baptism came about by mere men after the completion of the New Testament.

Consider this: The dead are to be buried, not the living. Many denominational churches erroneously teach that those being baptized are already alive spiritually (i.e., saved). Thus, they bury living people! The truth is, however, we are buried in the watery grave of baptism dead in sin and rise up a new creature (Col. 2:13).

Conversions in Acts

I find it interesting that every detailed conversion in the book of Acts mentions baptism. For instance, the Jews on Pentecost were baptized (2:41), the Samaritans were baptized (8:12), Simon was baptized (8:13), the eunuch was baptized (8:38), Saul of Tarsus was baptized (9:18), Cornelius was baptized (10:48), Lydia was baptized (16:15), the jailor was baptized (16:33), Crispus and the Corinthians were baptized (18:8), and the Ephesians were baptized (19:5). Would any dare say that baptism being mentioned in every detailed conversion in the book of Acts was mere coincidence? Hardly. Clearly baptism has an important part in the plan of salvation.

The conversions in Acts also reveal that rejoicing did not occur until after baptism (Acts 8:39; 16:34). That is because the burden of sin was not lifted prior to that time.

Questions on Lesson 2

1. What is the Scriptural pattern for salvation in Mark 16:16?

2. Explain how Catholicism and Protestantism change that pattern.

3. What was necessary to make redemption possible?

4. When does one come in contact with the blood of Christ?

5. Peter said we are to be baptized "for the remission of sins." Explain the meaning of the word "for" in that verse.

6. Does the account of the thief on the cross teach us that baptism is not necessary for salvation? Explain.

7. Why were believers baptized immediately in the New Testament?

8. Several times in the book of Acts, Luke tells of households being converted. Does this justify infant baptism? Explain.

9. What is significant about baptism being an immersion?

Lesson 3

Plan of Salvation (Part 3)

In this third and final lesson on the plan of salvation, we will notice a few more points to help wrap up this vital topic.

Love Obeys

Some argue that baptism and other commandments do not have to be obeyed because of love. They say, "All that really matters is that we love God." However, they fail to realize that true love obeys the commandments of God. Jesus said so in John 14: "If ye love me, keep my commandments" (v. 15), "He that hath my commandments, and keepeth them, he it is that loveth me" (v. 21), "If a man love me, he will keep my words" (v. 23), "He that loveth me not keepth not my sayings" (v. 24). John declared, "For this is the love of God, that we keep his commandments: and his commandments are not grievous" (1 Jn. 5:3) and "This is love, that we walk after his commandments" (2 Jn. 6). Those who truly love God are those who keep His commandments. Love obeys!

Obedience to the gospel is essential to man's salvation. "But God be thanked, that ye were the servants of sin, but ye have obeyed from the heart that form of doctrine which was delivered you. Being then made free from sin, ye became the servants of righteousness" (Rom. 6:17-18). "And to you who are troubled rest with us, when the Lord Jesus shall be revealed from heaven with his mighty angels, In flaming fire taking vengeance on them that know not God, and that obey not the gospel of our Lord Jesus Christ: Who shall be punished with everlasting destruction from the presence of the Lord, and from the glory of his power" (2 Thess. 1:7-9). "And being made perfect, he became the author of eternal salvation unto all them that obey him" (Heb. 5:9). "Seeing ye have purified your souls in obeying the truth through the Spirit unto unfeigned love of the brethren, see that ye love one another with a pure heart fervently" (1 Pet. 1:22). "Blessed are they that do his commandments, that they may have right to the tree of life, and may enter in through the gates into the city" (Rev. 22:14). If one does not obey, he is not saved.

The Perfect Plan

God loved the world so much that He gave us the perfect sacrifice and the perfect plan of salvation. One must hear the gospel, believe the gospel, repent of his sins, confess his faith, and be baptized into Christ. After that, he must continue to live for Christ all the days of his life by growing in the faith (2 Pet. 3:18), assembling with the saints (Heb. 10:25), continuing in prayer (1 Thess. 5:17), restoring the fallen (Jam. 5:19-20), and defending the truth (Jude 3).

Salvation
Baptized
Confess
Repent
Believe
Hear

At this juncture I submit an article by the late A.C. Grider. He wrote about a debate he had with a denominational preacher on the plan of salvation. It is appropriate here.

> I have met W.T. Russell (Baptist) four times in public debate. He is an artful dodger and developed into a fine debater so far as defending Baptist Doctrine is concerned. The first debate in which I ever had a part was with Russell and it was his first attempt at public debating. The discussion took place in the courthouse at Lafayette, Tennessee. There were several interesting incidents during the discussion. I will relate one.
>
> The subject for the debate was the "Plan of Salvation," and I was affirming that baptism is essential to salvation. Desiring to make things as simple as possible, I displayed a large chart with the "steps" in becoming a child of God clearly indicated. The chart consisted of a stairway with the steps labeled with the letters H, B, R, C, and B. I showed in my argument that in order to become a child of God, one must: 1. Hear the gospel, 2. Believe the gospel, 3. Repent of sins, 4. Confess Christ as Lord, and 5. Be baptized for

remission of sins. I cited appropriate scriptures for each point and emphasized every scripture. I suggested, with emphasis, that if Russell ever gave us any kind of an example of one becoming a Christian, his example would of necessity include these five points.

Russell countered with the idea that one is saved by "believing on Christ." I replied that he was right but that believing on Christ included these five points. I pressed him to show how one believed on Christ. He said one believed on Christ by trusting in him for salvation. Again I agreed that he was right but I pointed out that he was still using general terms. I suggested that he tell us how to trust in Christ and that if he did, he would necessarily include my five steps. I chided him to tell the audience HOW to trust in Christ. He said one trusted in Christ when he took Christ as his personal saviour. I agreed that he was right but I insisted that when he told us how to take Christ as saviour he would still have to come to my five steps. I called upon him to tell us exactly how to take Christ as saviour. He replied that one takes Christ when he believes on him. I showed the audience that Russell was simply "running around in circles." He said believe and you believe by trusting, and you trust by taking Christ, and you take Christ when you believe. I kept insisting that he spell out HOW to believe, trust, take, and again believe. I pressed him so hard to give us an example of becoming a child of God that he finally exploded and said, "I am going to give an example of trusting in Christ and make it so plain that it will soak into Grider's thick head." So he proceeded to give the example. To my surprise and to the surprise of everybody present, he said, "I have heard of the Mayo Clinic at Rochester, Minnesota. I believe it is there and that it can do a good work. But I have never trusted in the clinic. But if I leave here and go to Rochester and tell them of my confidence in them, and crawl on the table and submit to an operation, then will I have trusted in the clinic."

By the time he had finished with his speech the old debaters among the Baptists (and perhaps 25 Baptist preachers were present) had their heads in their laps almost. I accepted his example of trusting in Christ. I then showed that 1. His hearing about the clinic corresponded with my hearing about Christ, that 2. His believing the clinic was there corresponded with my believing that Jesus was the Christ, that 3. His leaving and going to Minnesota corresponded with my repenting, 4. His telling them of his confidence in them corresponded to my confession of Jesus Christ as the Son of God, and that 5. His submitting to an operation corresponded to my being baptized for the remission of sins. For good measure, I showed that Paul said we were "operated on" in baptism (Col. 2:12-13). It was a devastating blow to Russell and he never recovered from it. At the conclusion of the debate I heard Russell complain to one of his brethren, "What makes me so mad is that many of my own brethren seem to think more of old Grider than they do of me."

I have used Russell's example many times in teaching the truth on the plan of salvation. It is indeed a perfect illustration in trusting. You may be able to use it sometime in teaching a neighbor or friend.

Brother Grider converted many people to Jesus Christ through public debates. He was never afraid or ashamed to defend the truth of the gospel. For that I am thankful.

The Holy Spirit

When one talks about salvation, he must mention the Holy Spirit. He revealed the truth of the gospel to the apostles (Jn. 16:13; 1 Cor. 2:12-13).

The Holy Spirit is part of the Godhead. He is called God (Acts 5:3-4) just as the Father (2 Pet. 1:17) and Son (Jn. 1:1) are called God. He is an eternal being (Heb. 9:14). He is omniscient, omnipotent, and omnipresent. He is described in scripture as being full of goodness, holiness, and truth.

The Holy Spirit is not an "it" or some "indefinable feeling." He is a person. He possesses all the characteristics of personage. He hears (Jn. 16:13), speaks (1 Tim. 4:1), teaches (Jn. 14:26), communes (2 Cor. 13:14), leads (Rom. 8:14), comforts (Acts 9:31), testifies (Jn. 15:26), and bears witness (Rom. 8:16). He can be lied to (Acts 5:3), grieved (Eph. 4:30), blasphemed (Matt. 12:31), resisted (Acts 7:51), quenched (1 Thess. 5:19), and despised (Heb. 10:29). He has a will (1 Cor. 12:11) and knowledge (1 Cor. 2:11). Notice that all of the above passages demonstrate that the Holy Spirit has the characteristics of personage.

The Holy Spirit is alive and active in the world today. He works through the Word. It is His means or medium of operation. Consider the chart below.

Holy Spirit	Word
Testifies (Jn. 15:26)	Testifies (Jn. 5:39)
Saves (Tit. 3:5)	Saves (Jam. 1:21)
Teaches (1 Cor. 2:13)	Teaches (2 Thess. 2:15)
Comforts (Acts 9:31)	Comforts (1 Thess. 4:18)
Sanctifies (1 Cor. 6:11)	Sanctifies (Jn. 17:17)
Reproves (Jn. 16:8)	Reproves (2 Tim. 3:16)

From the above chart we see that the Holy Spirit works through the Word. It is His instrument. He testifies — through the Word, saves — through the Word, teaches — through the Word, comforts — through the Word, sanctifies — through the Word, and reproves — through the Word. This point is further demonstrated in the fact that those who resisted the Word were said to have resisted the Holy Spirit (Acts 7:51).

Calvinists erroneously teach that before one can respond to the gospel and be saved, he must experience the "direct operation of the Holy Spirit" upon his heart. However, the scriptures are clear that we are brought to God by the Word, not by some supernatural experience separate and apart from it. "Believe...through their word" (Jn. 17:20), "Written, that ye might believe" (Jn. 20:31), "Faith comes by hearing...the word of God" (Rom. 10:17), "Begotten...through the gospel" (1 Cor. 4:15), "Called...by our gospel" (2 Thess. 2:14), "Begat...with the word of truth" (Jam. 1:18), "Born again...by the word of God" (1 Pet. 1:23).

Salvation & The Church

The Bible says that the saved are added to the church (Acts 2:47). Therefore, one cannot be saved and be outside of the church. Think about it. The church is the house of God (1 Tim. 3:15), and as such it includes and consists of all the children of God. The church is also the body of Christ (Col. 1:18), and as such it includes and consists of every member of Christ. Furthermore, we are reconciled in Christ — in the body (Eph. 2:16), called to peace in Christ — in the body (Col. 3:15), partakers of the promise in Christ — in the body (Eph. 3:6), and saved in Christ — in the body (Eph. 5:23). Indeed, Christ and the church share an intimate relationship. If a man is not in the church, he is not in Christ. Consider the chart below.

Christ	Church
Head (Col. 1:18)	Body (1 Cor. 12:27)
King (Rev. 17:14)	Kingdom (Col. 1:13)
Groom (2 Cor. 11:2)	Bride (2 Cor. 11:2)
Foundation (1 Cor. 3:11)	Building (1 Cor. 3:9)
Savior (2 Pet. 1:1)	Saved (Eph. 5:23)

Spiritual Blessings

All spiritual blessings are in Christ. Paul wrote, "Blessed be the God and Father of our Lord Jesus Christ, who hath blessed us with all spiritual blessings in heavenly places in Christ" (Eph. 1:3). These marvelous blessings include peace (Jn. 16:33), righteousness (2 Cor. 5:21), redemption (Eph. 1:7), forgiveness (Col. 1:14), grace (2 Tim. 2:1), salvation (2 Tim. 2:10), and eternal life (1 Jn. 5:11). We enter into Christ at the same time and in the same way that we enter into the church — through baptism (Rom. 6:3; 1 Cor. 12:13). Therefore, we must conclude that to be in Christ, where all the spiritual blessings are found, is to be in the church. If a man is not in the church, he is not in Christ!

Conclusion

John declared, "He that believeth on the Son hath everlasting life: and he that believeth not the Son shall not see life: but the wrath of God abideth on him" (Jn. 3:36). Faith in the Son of God is essential to salvation. We must understand, however, that saving faith is an obedient faith. It is a working faith. One must repent of his sins, confess his faith, and be baptized into Christ. Have you done that?

Questions on Lesson 3

1. If we love God, what will we do with regard to His commandments?

2. According to 2 Thessalonians 1:7-9, what two groups of people will be punished when the Lord returns?

3. What is God's perfect plan for salvation?

4. After obeying the gospel, what does God expect us to do?

5. What is the instrument by which the Holy Spirit operates today?

6. Calvinists believe that one cannot respond to the gospel and be saved apart from some "direct operation of the Holy Spirit." Explain how this is contrary to the scriptures.

7. When one is saved, to what is he added?

8. Can one be saved outside of the church? Explain.

9. What spiritual blessings are found in Christ?

10. How does one get into Christ?

Lesson 4

Work of the Church

The Lord has given the church a particular work to do. The work is threefold in nature: (1) benevolence for needy saints, (2) edification, and (3) evangelism. It is important that each part of the work be accomplished as set forth in the New Testament.

(1) **Benevolence.** The church is to provide benevolence for needy members. For instance, in Acts 6 we read about a problem that occurred in the church at Jerusalem. Some of the widows were being neglected in the daily service rendered to those in need. The Bible says, "And in those days, when the number of the disciples was multiplied, there arose a murmuring of the Grecians against the Hebrews, because their widows were neglected in the daily ministration. Then the twelve called the multitude of the disciples unto them, and said, It is not reason that we should leave the word of God, and serve tables. Wherefore, brethren, look ye out among you seven men of honest report, full of the Holy Ghost and wisdom, whom we may appoint over this business. But we will give ourselves continually to prayer, and to the ministry of the word. And the saying pleased the whole multitude and they chose Stephen, a man full of faith and of the Holy Ghost, and Philip, and Prochorus, and Nicanor, and Timon, and Parmenas, and Nicolas, a proselyte of Antioch: Whom they set before the apostles: and when they had prayed, they laid their hands on them" (vv. 1-6). Notice that the apostles recognized the responsibility the church had of caring for needy members. It was a duty that could not be ignored. Therefore, they had the congregation appoint seven men to carry out the work of benevolence.

In Acts 11, we read about a famine that was going to occur, in which the brethren in Judea would not be capable of providing for themselves. The Bible says, "And in these days came prophets from Jerusalem unto Antioch. And there stood up one of them named Agabus, and signified by the Spirit that there should be a great dearth throughout all the world; which came to pass in the days of Claudius Caesar. Then the disciples, every man according to his ability, determined to send relief unto the brethren which dwelt in Judea: Which also they did, and sent it to the elders by the hands of Barnabas and Saul" (vv. 27-30). Here is another example of benevolence. Since the Judean brethren would not be capable of providing for themselves during the dearth (famine), the brethren in other areas sent relief to the elders so that they could do *their own work* of benevolence.

In 1 Timothy 5, we have instruction concerning benevolence for needy members. The Bible says, "If any man or woman that believeth have widows, let them relieve them, and let not the church be charged; that it may relieve them that are widows indeed" (v. 16). Here we see that family members of the one in need have the primary responsibility of providing care. In such cases, Paul said, "let not the church be charged." The church should be focused on caring for those truly destitute and helpless — "widows indeed."

Limited Benevolence

As followers of the divine pattern, it is important for us to realize that the church can only help needy saints. Her work of benevolence is limited in nature (Acts 2:44-46; 4:32-35; 6:1-6; 11:27-30; Rom. 15:25-31; 1 Cor. 16:1-3; 2 Cor. 8:1-4, 13-14; 2 Cor. 9:1-15; 1 Tim. 5:16). It is not the work of the church to be a welfare agency for every needy person in the world. On the other hand, however, individual members can and should help as many as opportunity and means allow. Paul wrote, "As we have therefore opportunity, let us do good unto all men, especially unto them that are of the household of faith" (Gal. 6:10). God's children are to be charitable and generous people. They should have a heart of compassion that is eager to aid and assist those in need whenever possible. The story of the Good Samaritan is a great example of such compassion (Lk. 10:25-37). We must not confuse the difference between what the church can do and what the individual can do in terms of benevolence.

It is necessary to address the extent of benevolence. As stated above, the church has an obligation to help needy members. This is a responsibility that cannot be overlooked. However, there may be cases that do not warrant such help. For instance, a member may think he is in need because he wants a new car or a bigger house, but that would not qualify as benevolence from the church treasury. Benevolence is not designed to sustain a luxurious lifestyle. It is for absolute necessities. Furthermore, the church is not expected to help those who are physically able to work and provide for themselves but will not do so. Paul wrote, "If any would not work, neither should he eat" (2 Thess. 3:10) and "If any provide not for his own, and specially for those of his own house, he hath denied the faith, and is worse than an infidel" (1 Tim. 5:8). Laziness should be rebuked, not supported by the treasury.

(2) **Edification.** To "edify" means to build up. It is the work of the church to edify, or build up, every member in the faith (Eph. 4:11-16). Paul wrote, "Let all things be done unto edifying" (1 Cor. 14:26).

Can you imagine a baby that never matures beyond milk? He would suffer from severe malnutrition and eventually die. The same is true with spiritual babies. They must progress from milk to strong meat in order to stay healthy. In fact, the Hebrews writer condemned those who were not maturing in the faith and called them to deeper devotion. He wrote, "For when for the time ye ought to be teachers, ye have need that one teach you again which be the first principles of the oracles of God; and are become such as have need of milk, and not strong meat. For every one that useth milk is unskillful in the word of righteousness: for he is a babe. But strong meat belongeth to them that are of full age, even those who by reason of use have their senses exercised to discern both good and evil" (Heb. 5:12-14). Notice the contrast between milk and strong meat, babe and full age. Spiritual development is essential to the well-being of Christians. We must grow in the faith (1 Pet. 2:2; 2 Pet. 3:18).

Edification is not accomplished by erecting gymnasiums and fellowship halls, but by the preaching and teaching of God's Word. For instance, when Paul gave his farewell address to the elders at Ephesus, he said, "And now, brethren, I commend you to God, and to *the word of his grace*, which is able to build you up, and to give you an inheritance among all them which are sanctified" (Acts 20:32, emphasis mine). Notice that "the word of grace" is the source of our edification. We are built up as we study the scriptures and apply them to our lives.

When brethren miss Bible class, they are doing themselves a grave injustice. Such classes provide a great opportunity for growth and development. I dare say that more is learned in the Bible class setting than in the worship service. Christians who are committed to growing in the faith will take advantage of Bible class.

(3) **Evangelism.** The primary mission of the church is that of evangelism. She is the "pillar and ground of the truth" (1 Tim. 3:15). She is to be a beacon of hope and life to the community. It is through evangelism that souls are saved and the borders of the kingdom increased. "To teach God's word and to preach the gospel of His Son to dying humanity is the noblest work on this earth. You may feed and clothe humanity and provide for them good homes, but if you fail to induce them to obey the gospel, they will die and land in hell at last. The church is God's great missionary agency for proclaiming to a lost, ruined, and recreant race of mankind the hope of everlasting bliss. Any church, therefore, that is not interested, is not active, that is not doing something for the spread of the gospel among the denizens of this earth

is not a distant relative of the church Christ died to establish" (*Hardeman's Tabernacle Sermons*, Vol. V, N.B. Hardeman, p. 56).

God's Word is the seed (Lk. 8:11; 1 Pet 1:23). Seed produces life. The Word bears the same relationship to the production of faith in the spiritual realm that the material seed bears to the production of fruit in the physical realm. The Bible says, "So then faith cometh by hearing, and hearing by the word of God" (Rom. 10:17). Faith cannot grow in the hearts and souls of men until the seed has been planted (Ps. 119:50). Therefore, the church must be hard at work planting the seed of the gospel.

The Thessalonian church was commended for her efforts in propagating the gospel. Paul wrote, "For from you sounded out the word of the Lord, not only in Macedonia and Achaia, but also in every place your faith to God-ward is spread abroad; so that we need not to speak any thing" (1 Thess. 1:8). Notice that the congregation was praised for sounding out the Word of the Lord. To "sound out" means to ring out. It denotes a thunderous noise. Every church of Christ should be busy ringing out the glorious gospel.

It is not good for churches to have large sums of money just sitting dormant in the bank. That may sound crazy, but it is true. The Lord's money should be put to use in spreading the gospel. Sponsor a television program, purchase time on the radio, support gospel preachers, put advertisements in the newspaper — just do something to get the message out!

Power of Gospel

God's Word is extremely powerful. It pricks hearts and changes lives. In fact, the word "power" in Romans 1:16 comes from the Greek word *dunamis*, from which we get our English word dynamite. The gospel is God's dynamite to save! Consider the following chart.

Cause	Effect
Word	Believe (Jn. 17:20)
Written	Believe (Jn. 20:31)
Heard	Pricked (Acts 2:37)
Heard	Believed (Acts 4:4)

Cause	Effect
Spake	Believed (Acts 14:1)
Hearing	Believed (Acts 18:8)
Gospel	Saved (Rom. 1:16)
Word	Faith (Rom. 10:17)
Preaching	Saved (1 Cor. 1:21)
Gospel	Begotten (1 Cor. 4:15)
Gospel	Called (2 Thess. 2:14)
Word	Begat (Jam. 1:18)
Word	Saved (Jam. 1:21)
Word	Born Again (1 Pet. 1:23)

Notice that the Holy Spirit operates through the Word. It is the means or medium by which sinners are convicted of their sins and converted to Christ (Heb. 4:12). For instance, would any deny that the Spirit was working in the conversion of the Jews in Acts 2? Surely not. Yet we see that He worked through the Word: "Began to speak" (v. 4), "heard them speak" (v. 6), "hearken to my words" (v. 14), "hear these words" (v. 22), "when they heard this" (v. 37), "Peter said' (v. 38), "with many other words" (v. 40), "gladly received his word" (v. 41). The Jews were converted by the Spirit through the Word.

Losing Focus

When the church takes her eye off evangelism, she drifts away from the harbor of heaven. Many churches of Christ have been led into apostasy because they exchanged the *saving* gospel for the *social* gospel. They have taken on the ridiculous role of providing entertainment and recreation. It is not the work of the church to furnish games and gimmicks. She is not responsible for karate classes and daycare services, rafting trips and bowling leagues, soccer clinics and youth rallies, financial seminars and basketball tournaments. The Bible says, "For the kingdom of God is not meat and drink; but righteousness, and peace, and joy in the Holy Ghost" (Rom. 14:17). The mission of the church is spiritual in nature, not carnal. "Again I say to you, with caution and thought, that it is not the work of the church to furnish entertainment for the members. And yet many churches have drifted into such effort. They enlarge their basements, put in all kinds of gymnastic apparatus, and make every sort of an appeal to the young people of the congregation. I have never read anything in the Bible that indicated to me that such was a part of the work of the church. I am wholly ignorant of any scripture that even points in that direction" (*Hardeman's Tabernacle Sermons*, Vol. V, N.B. Hardeman, p. 50). "It is not the mission of the church to furnish amusement for the world or even for its own members. Innocent amusement in proper proportion has its place in the life of all normal persons, but it is not the business of the church to furnish it. For the church to turn aside from its divine work to furnish amusement and recreation is to pervert its mission. If the church will discharge its duty in preaching the gospel, in edifying its members, and helping the worthy poor, it will not have desire or the time merely to amuse and entertain" (*Torch*, Vol. I, B.C. Goodpasture, No. 2, p. 26, August 1950). Amen.

3 Reasons Why Social Gospel is Wrong

It perverts the nature of the mission of Christ. Jesus Christ came to save the lost, not to entertain people. His appeal was spiritual in nature, not carnal (Matt. 1:21; Lk. 19:10; 1 Tim. 1:15). The social gospel puts the focus on fun, food, and frolic. Salvation is overshadowed by recreation.

It underestimates the power of the gospel. The gospel is fully capable of bringing the lost to Jesus. It has sufficient power to prick hearts and save souls (Rom. 1:16; 1 Cor. 1:21; Jam. 1:21). The truth does not need a basketball goal to score conversions for Christ.

It markets the church. The social gospel appeals to man's carnal desires. Whatever man *needs* is replaced by whatever man *wants*. For instance, churches now offer everything from weight loss programs to dating clubs. Surely one can see that such marketing schemes appeal to the appetites of the flesh, not the soul.

We live in a time when gospel meetings are being shortened, if not canceled completely. This is a big mistake. Although it may be an inconvenience for some members to attend all five or six nights of a meeting, we must not lose focus of the opportunity we are providing for the people around us. If one lost soul is able to hear the gospel of Jesus Christ preached during a meeting, every ounce of energy put forth is worth it. I dare any Christian to disagree. We need more preaching in the world today, not less!

Evangelism & Human Institutions

The church is all-sufficient. She has the perfect builder, the perfect blueprint, the perfect head, the perfect law, and the perfect mission. She does not need the help of human institutions.

"Human societies to take over and do the work of the church which the Lord built his church to do are spiritual forgeries for they are unauthorized in the scriptures. The only thing that God ever built in the way of religious organizations is the church. He gave it order and arrangement that it might accomplish his will...The maze of Missionary Societies, Education Societies, etc., did not exist and the man does not live that can find authority for their existence today in the scriptures. They are human and not divine. They are spiritual forgeries and those who promote them will stand condemned" (*Gospel Guardian*, Roy Cogdill, June 16, 1966). The church is God's one and only missionary society! Amen.

Conclusion

It is very important that disciples have a clear understanding of the work of the church. It includes benevolence for needy saints, edification, and evangelism. I was taught to remember this threefold work by thinking about the bumblebee (BEE). Needless to say, it stuck. Maybe it will stick with you too.

Questions on Lesson 4

1. What is the threefold work of the church?

2. In Acts 6, what did the Jerusalem church do to provide help for the needy widows among them?

3. When the brethren in Antioch determined to send aid to the needy brethren in Jerusalem, to whom did they send money?

4. Who has the primary responsibility to care for the needy (1 Tim. 5:16)?

5. What group of people are individual Christians authorized to help, but churches are not?

6. Explain the sort of help that is to be provided in the work of benevolence.

7. What does edification mean?

8. What is the goal of edification?

9. How is edification accomplished?

10. What might a church do to edify its members?

11. What is the primary mission of the church?

12. What is the "seed" that is planted by the church?

13. Through what does the Holy Spirit operate?

14. What is the "social gospel" and how is it different than the gospel of Christ?

15. Why is the social gospel wrong?

16. Why are human institutions unauthorized to do the work of evangelism?

36 | The Simple Truth

Lesson 5

Worship of the Church (Part 1)

Man is by nature a worshiping creature. Every known civilization to live upon the face of the earth has had an inherent desire to worship something. Where does such a desire originate? Why does mankind have an innate yearning to worship? Could it be that God made us that way? There can be no doubt. Man was created to worship God.

Authorized Worship Only

God has always expected His people to worship Him in the manner He prescribed. He will not tolerate unauthorized worship. For instance, when Cain and Abel brought their offerings to the Lord, one was accepted while the other was rejected. The Bible says, "And in the process of time it came to pass, that Cain brought of the fruit of the ground an offering unto the Lord. And Abel, he also brought of the firstlings of his flock and of the fat thereof. And the Lord had respect unto Abel and to his offering: But unto Cain and his offering he had not respect. And Cain was wroth, and his countenance fell" (Gen. 4:3-5). Notice these men were worshiping the same God, but were not received the same by Him. Why is that? Although we do not have all the specifics about this situation, we do know that Abel offered his sacrifice "by faith" (Heb. 11:4). Since faith comes by hearing the Word of God (Rom. 10:17), we can safely conclude that at some point God had given them instructions for worship. Abel obeyed the instructions of God; Cain did not.

In Levitucus 10, we have another example of unauthorized worship. Nadab and Abihu, the sons of Aaron, offered profane fire before the Lord and were destroyed. The Bible says, "And Nadab and Abihu, the sons of Aaron, took either of them his censer, and put fire therein, and put incense thereon, and offered strange fire before the Lord, which he commanded them not. And there went out fire from the Lord, and devoured them, and they died before the Lord" (vv. 1-2). Notice that these men were worshiping the right God, but did so in the wrong way. They worshiped Him with "strange fire" in a way He "commanded them not." Therefore, they were punished. From this tragic event, we learn that our worship must be according to God's will (Col. 3:17).

In 1 Kings 12, we read about a king who instituted a new form of worship. The Bible says, "Whereupon the king took counsel, and made two calves of God, and said unto them, It is too much for you to go up to Jerusalem: behold thy gods, O Israel, which brought thee up out of the land of Egypt. And he set the one in Bethel, and the other put he in Dan. And this thing became a sin; for the people went to worship before the one, even unto Dan. And he made a house of high places, and made priests of the lowest of the people, which were not of the sons of Levi. And Jeroboam ordained a feast in the eighth month, on the fifteenth day of the month, like unto the feast that is in Judah, and he offered upon the altar. So did he in Bethel, sacrificing unto the calves that he had made: and he placed in Bethel the priests of the high places which he had made. So he offered upon the altar which he had made in Bethel the fifteenth day of the eighth month, even in the month which he had devised of his own heart; and ordained a feast unto the children of Israel: and he offered upon the altar, and burnt incense" (vv. 28-33). Notice that Jeroboam substituted the Lord's way for his own way. He created golden calves to be worshiped as gods in Bethel and Dan, ordained priests that were not of Levi, and instituted a new religious feast in the eighth month that rivaled the Feast of Tabernacles in the seventh month. These things were devised in his own heart (v. 33). What was the result? He lost his kingdom and was eventually struck dead by the Lord (2 Chron. 13:20).

Many people today suffer from "Jeroboamitis." They have substituted the Lord's way for their own way. This point will be developed in detail later in the chapter.

When Jesus spoke to the woman at the well, He told her that true worshipers must worship God "in spirit and in truth" (Jn. 4:24). This means that our worship is both internal and external. It must consist of the right attitude (in spirit), and it must be according to divine revelation (in truth). Let us consider the pattern for worship as revealed in the New Testament.

Pattern for Worship

(1) **Singing.** The Lord's people are to sing praises in worship. Paul wrote, "I will pray with the spirit, and I will pray with the understanding also: I will sing with the spirit, and I will sing with the understanding also" (1 Cor. 14:15). There can be no doubting or denying that the early disciples sang songs in service to God (Heb. 2:12).

Instrumental Music

When Naaman was commanded to dip in the Jordan River (2 Kgs. 5:10), was he at liberty to dip in the Nile River or Euphrates River instead? No. By specifying the Jordan River, every other river was excluded. The same is true with our song service. By specifying singing, every other kind of music is excluded. We are not to hum, drum, strum, pluck, or play. We are simply to offer "the fruit of our lips" (Heb. 13:15). "Musical instruments in celebrating the praises of God would be no more suitable than the burning of incense, the lighting up of lamps, and the restoration of the other shadows of the law. The Papists, therefore, have foolishly borrowed this, as well as many other things, from the Jews" (*Calvin's Commentary*, Vol. IV, Ps. 33, John Calvin, p. 539). "What a degradation to supplant the intelligent song of the whole congregation by the theatrical prettinesses of a quartette, the refined niceties of a choir, or the blowing off of wind from inanimate bellows and pipes! We might as well pray by machinery as praise by it" (*The Treasury of David*, Vol. I, Ps. 42, Charles H. Spurgeon, p. 272). "Staunch old Baptists in former times would as soon have tolerated the Pope of Rome in their pulpits as an organ in their galleries" (*50 Years Among the Baptists*, David Benedict, p. 283). "Although Josephus tells of the wonderful effects produced in the Temple by the use of instruments, the first Christians were of too spiritual a fibre to substitute lifeless instruments for or to use them to accompany the human voice. Clement of Alexandria severely condemns the use of instruments even at Christian banquets" (*The Catholic Encyclopedia*, Vol. X, p. 651).

Making Melody

Some have argued that the words "making melody" (*psallo*) in Ephesians 5:19 authorize the use of mechanical instruments in the church. While it is true that at one time the word suggested plucking a stringed instrument, by the time of its use in the New Testament, it simply meant to sing. Every major translation bears that out. Consider the quotes from some well-respected lexicographers below.

> Liddell-Scott: "sing...NT"
> Mounce: "in NT to sing praises"
> Green: "in N.T. to sing praises"
> Trenchard: "to sing, sing praise"
> Thayer: "in the N.T. to sing a hymn, to celebrate the praises of God in song"
> Arndt-Gingrich: "sing, sing praise"

Sophocles: "to chant, sing religious hymns"

If the passage did indeed authorize the use of mechanical instruments in the church, then every member would have to play one. The truth is, however, the words "making melody" simply meant to sing.

Aids & Additions

It is important for us to understand the difference between aids and additions. Aids help in fulfilling the command, without changing the nature of the command. Additions, on the other hand, change the very nature of the command. For instance, Noah was commanded to build an ark of gopher wood (Gen. 6:14). In fulfilling that command he used hammers, saws, and other tools. Did those things change the nature of the command? No. They simply aided him in fulfilling the command to build an ark of gopher wood. However, had Noah used oak or cherry in place of the gopher wood, he would have changed the very nature of the command. Hence, those things would be unauthorized additions.

Church Buildings. We are commanded to assemble (Heb. 10:25). A church building is authorized because it aids in fulfilling the command to assemble, without changing the nature of the command.

Overhead Projectors. We are commanded to teach (2 Tim. 2:2). An overhead projector is authorized because it aids in fulfilling the command to teach, without changing the nature of the command.

Collection Baskets. We are commanded to give (1 Cor. 16:2). A collection basket is authorized because it aids in fulfilling the command to give, without changing the nature of the command.

Baptismal Pools. We are commanded to baptize (Matt. 28:19). A baptismal pool is authorized because it aids in fulfilling the command to baptize, without changing the nature of the command.

Songbooks. We are commanded to sing (Eph. 5:19). A songbook is authorized because it aids in fulfilling the command to sing, without changing the nature of the command.

Gymnasiums. We are *not* commanded to provide recreation in the New Testament. Therefore, gymnasiums do not classify as aids. They are additions.

Mechanical Instruments. We are *not* commanded to play music in the New Testament. Therefore, mechanical instruments do not classify as aids. They are additions.

I hope you can now distinguish between an authorized aid and an unauthorized addition. There is a clear difference. Consider the chart below.

Command	Aid	Addition
Immerse	Baptistry	Sprinkling
Sing	Songbook	Instrument
Assemble	Building	Gymnasium
Lord's Supper	Plates/Cups	Burgers/Sprite

Solos and Choirs

The singing of the church is to be congregational. God has revealed that every member is to participate in the song service, not just a select few. Paul wrote, "Speaking one to another in psalms and hymns and spiritual songs" (Eph. 5:19, ASV) and "Teaching and admonishing one another with psalms and hymns and spiritual songs" (Col. 3:16, ASV). Notice that our singing is to be a reciprocal action. The terms "one to another" and "one another" are grammatically classified as reciprocal pronouns. They represent an interchange of action. Every member should participate in every song.

While not our standard of authority, ancient historians acknowledge that the singing of the early church was congregational. Saints simultaneously sang praises to God. "The prevailing mode of singing during the first three centuries was congregational. The whole congregation united their voices in the sacred song of praise...The most ancient and most common mode of singing was confessedly for the whole assembly" (*Ancient Christianity Exemplified*, pp. 329, 330). "The song, a form of prayer, in the festive dress of poetry and elevated language of inspiration, raising the congregation to the highest pitch of devotion, and giving it a part in the heavenly harmonies of the saints" (*History of the Christian Church*, Vol. I, p. 463). "In the early church, the whole congregation joined in the singing" (The Ancient Church, pp. 193, 423). "From the apostolic age singing was always a part of divine service, in which the whole body of the church joined together; and it was the decay of this practice that first brought the order of singers into the church" (*Cyclopedia of Biblical, Theological, And Ecclesiastical Literature*, Vol. IX, p. 776). Even historians acknowledge that the singing of the church is to be congregational.

Soloists and choirs cause the church to engage in worship by proxy. A select few members sing, while others sit quietly. Such is not the pattern of the New Testament. Every saint is to sing praises to God.

(2) **Preaching.** The church is in the business of saving souls. She is to be a launching pad for the proclamation of God's Word (1 Thess. 1:8). Our worship service should include wholesome preaching and teaching.

Evangelists are commanded to "preach the word" (2 Tim. 4:2). Though this should go without saying, it most certainly needs to be said in view of some current trends among the people of God. Sermons nowadays are watered-down and sugarcoated. They are depleted of scripture and inflated with cute stories and funny anecdotes. It ought not to be that way. We need to get back to good-old-fashioned book, chapter, and verse preaching.

Paul's Preaching

While in custody at Caesarea, Paul was visited by Felix, the procurator of Judea, and his wife Drusilla. The Bible says, "And after certain days, when Felix came with his wife Drusilla which was a Jewess, he sent for Paul, and heard him concerning the faith in Christ. And as he reasoned of righteousness, temperance, and judgment to come, Felix trembled, and answered, Go thy way for this time; when I have a convenient season, I will call for thee" (Acts 24:24-25). Felix was a very powerful person. He had the authority to release Paul or to have him executed. Yet Paul preached a sermon to the procurator that was "terrifying" (ASV).

Now why did Paul preach on righteousness, temperance (or self-control), and judgment to come? Have you ever thought about it? What was he thinking? Paul preached on those things because they were exactly what Felix needed to hear. According to Josephus, a Jewish historian, Felix had no right to Drusilla. They were living in an adulterous relationship. He records, "While Felix was procurator of Judea, he saw Drusilla, and fell in love with her; for she did indeed exceed all other women in beauty, and he sent to her a person whose name was Simon, one of his friends, a Jew he was, and by birth a Cypriot, and one who pretended to be a magician; and endeavored to persuade her to forsake her present husband, and marry him; and promised, that if she would not refuse him, he would make her a happy woman" (*The Works of Josephus*, pp. 533-534). Paul preached what was needed!

When Paul traveled to Athens and other cities filled with idolatry he preached on the one true living God. Were they ear-tickling sermons? No. Did his messages win him any popularity contests? No. In fact, the craftsmen at Ephesus, who made their livelihood in idolatry, enraged the community to riot against Paul (Acts 19:23-41). Yet he never wavered in his preaching because it was what they needed to hear.

We need men in the pulpit today who will call sin "sin." We need preachers who will preach against abortion, homosexuality, immodesty, drunkenness, fornication, divorce, institutionalism, and denominationalism. We need preachers with the courage and conviction to oppose even brethren who "bring in damnable heresies" and "overthrow the faith of some."

We need men who will preach on the one true church. Too many among us act as if they are ashamed of the church and its distinctive nature. They say we need to "preach more Christ, and less church." How can that be done? How can you preach the groom and not the bride? How can you preach the king and not the kingdom? How can you preach the foundation and not the house? How can you preach the savior and not the saved? How can you preach the head and not the body? Such is an impossible task. To preach Christ is to preach the church (Acts 8:5, 12). Preachers need to tell people about the one true church of our Lord.

This is not to say that preachers should be rude or impolite. Such behavior is counterproductive to the cause of Christ. We are told to "speak the truth in love" (Eph. 4:15). However, there is no excuse for preachers to avoid issues of importance just because it might offend someone in the pew. Tell them what they need to hear. Paul did!

Questions on Lesson 5

1. Why has every civilization had some form of worship?

2. What does it mean that Abel offered his sacrifice "by faith"?

3. Why did God not accept the offering of Nadab and Abihu?

4. What five acts make up our pattern for worship?

5. Explain why instrumental music is unauthorized in worship.

6. Explain the difference between an *aid* and an *addition*.

7. Why is singing to be done by the congregation and not by soloists or choirs?

8. Explain the difference in preaching what people *need* to hear and what they *want* to hear. Which should characterize our preaching?

Lesson 6

Worship of the Church (Part 2)

In this lesson we will continue where we left off in the previous lesson as we consider the various acts of worship.

(3) **Communion.** On the night He was betrayed, Jesus instituted the Lord's Supper (Matt. 26:17-26; Mk. 14:12-25; Lk. 22:7-30). This act of worship is designed to commemorate the death of Christ until He comes again. Paul wrote, "For I received of the Lord that which also I delivered unto you, That the Lord Jesus the same night in which he was betrayed took bread: And when he had given thanks, he brake it, and said, Take, eat: this is my body, which is broken for you; this do in remembrance of me. After the same manner also he took the cup, when he had supped, saying, This cup is the new testament in my blood; this do ye, as oft as ye drink it, in remembrance of me. For as often as ye eat this bread, and drink this cup, ye do show the Lord's death till he come" (1 Cor. 11:23-26). Notice that the unleavened bread and fruit of the vine represent the body and blood of Christ. They are emblematic of the sacrifice He made on our behalf.

Christians need to appreciate the sacredness of communion. It is not something to be done haphazardly or slipshod. Partakers should meditate upon what they are doing, and why they are doing it. Paul also said, "Wherefore whosoever shall eat this bread, and drink this cup of the Lord, unworthily, shall be guilty of the body and blood of the Lord. But let a man examine himself, and so eat of that bread, and drink of that cup. For he that eateth and drinketh unworthily, eateth and drinketh damnation to himself, not discerning the Lord's body" (vv. 27-29). To "examine" means to prove or to test. Christians should examine themselves before partaking of the Lord's Supper.

Elements

The Lord's Supper consists of unleavened bread and fruit of the vine. We know that the bread is to be unleavened because Jesus instituted the Lord's Supper during the feast of unleavened bread (Matt. 26:17). There would not have been any leaven in the house during that time (Ex. 12:19). The fruit of the vine is unfermented grape juice.

Day

The early disciples broke bread "upon the first day of the week" (Acts 20:7). Whereas the old covenant placed special significance on the seventh day, the new covenant places special significance on the first day. It was on the first day of the week that Jesus was raised from the dead, the church of Christ was established, and Christians assembled to give of their means. Sunday is the authorized time for the church to partake of the Lord's Supper.

It is striking that Luke, in Acts 20:7, makes it a point to specify the day in which the disciples came together to break bread. It is not likely that he did so by mere coincidence. The early church assembled on the first day of the week to partake of the Lord's Supper. "This passage shows that the first day of the week was the day in which the disciples broke the loaf" (*Commentary on Acts*, J.W. McGarvey, p. 179). "Showing thus that this day was then observed by Christians as holy time... evidently to celebrate the Lord's supper...It is probable that the apostles and early Christians celebrated the Lord's Supper on every Lord's day" (Barnes Notes on Acts, Albert Barnes, p. 288). "We have here the purpose of their gathering together on the first day of the week. It was to observe the Lord's Supper. In passing, people who do not have the Lord's Supper weekly in this age have deprived themselves of one of the very purposes for meeting together on the first day of the week" (*New Testament History* — Acts, Gareth L. Reese, p. 734).

Some argue that because Acts 20:7 does not say "every" first day of the week the church is not obligated to observe the Lord's Supper weekly. Such reasoning is illogical. For instance, God commanded the Jews to observe the Sabbath in Exodus 20:8. It says, "Remember the Sabbath day, to keep it holy." Notice that it does not say "every" Sabbath. Does that mean the Jews could skip a few? Were the Jews free to have a monthly Sabbath observance instead of a weekly one? The very thought is absurd. We all recognize that the command to keep holy the Sabbath would include every Sabbath even though it does not use the word "every." The same is true with the Lord's Supper. We are to observe it every Sunday.

Consider this: If Acts 20:7 said "first month of the year," it would imply an annual observance. If it said "first week of the month," it would imply a monthly observance. It says "first day of the week," therefore implying a weekly observance!

Place

The New Testament pattern not only authorizes the day for eating the Lord's Supper, it also authorizes the place — in the assembly. The early disciples "came together to break bread" (Acts 20:7). Consider the context of 1 Corinthians 11:

"Ye come together" (v. 17)
"When ye come together in the church" (v. 18)
"When ye come together therefore into one place" (v. 20)
"When ye come together to eat" (v. 33)
"That ye come not together unto condemnation" (v. 34)

Christians are to eat the Lord's Supper in the assembly. It is an act of worship that is to be observed collectively (Acts 2:42). If a brother is in a hospital or nursing home and cannot assemble with the saints, he is not required to eat the Lord's Supper.

Lord's Supper & Common Meal

Some seem to think that the Lord's Supper should be a common meal. Not so. We have a clear distinction made between the two in the New Testament (Acts 2:42, 46). In fact, Paul wrote, "Have ye not houses to eat and to drink in? Or despise ye the church of God, and shame them that have not? What shall I say to you? Shall I praise you in this? I praise you not" (1 Cor. 11:22) and said, "If any man hunger, let him eat at home, that ye come not together unto condemnation" (1 Cor. 11:34). Hence, the Lord's Supper is not designed to be a common meal. Eat your common meals "at home."

(4) **Giving.** The Mosaic Law required the people to give a tithe, or tenth (Lev. 27:30; 1 Sam. 8:15). Such is not the case for Christians. The New Testament does not specify a particular percentage. It simply tells us to give as we have prospered (1 Cor. 16:2) and as we have purposed in our hearts (2 Cor. 9:7). Consider the following passage both times.

> **1 Corinthians 16:2** — "Upon the first day of the week (when) let every one of you (who) lay by him in store, as God hath prospered him (how), that there be no gatherings when I come."

1 Corinthians 16:2 — "Upon the first day of the week (regularly) let every one of you (personally) lay by him in store, as God hath prospered him (proportionately), that there be no gatherings when I come."

Christians should give liberally to the Lord. It should be a sacrificial offering. Who can forget the story of the poor widow in Luke 21? The Bible says, "And he looked up, and saw the rich men casting their gifts into the treasury. And he saw also a certain poor widow casting in thither two mites. And he said, Of a truth I say unto you, that this poor widow hath cast in more than they all: For all these have of their abundance cast in unto the offerings of God: but she of her penury hath cast in all the living that she had" (vv. 1-4). Though the poor widow gave far less than the rich men, the Lord said she "cast in more than they all" because she gave sacrificially. So should we. I fear that too many Christians are stingy with their money. They are so carnally minded that it is hard for them to give liberally to the Lord. I pray such people will heed the following passages.

Ecclesiastes 5:15 — "As he came forth of his mother's womb, naked shall he return to go as he came, and shall take nothing of his labor, which he may carry away in his hand."

Matthew 16:26 — "For what is a man profited, if he shall gain the whole world, and lose his own soul? Or what shall a man give in exchange for his soul?"

Luke 12:15 — "Take heed, and beware of covetousness: for a man's life consisteth not in the abundance of the things which he possesseth."

1 Timothy 6:7 — "For we brought nothing into this world, and it is certain we can carry nothing out."

1 Timothy 6:10 — "For the love of money is the root of all evil: which while some coveted after, they have erred from the faith, and pierced themselves through with many sorrows."

We have all heard the expression "You can't take it with you." How true that is. Do not allow the temporal treasures and fleeting fortunes of this world to keep you from inheriting heavenly riches (Matt. 6:19-20; Lk. 12:16-21). Give liberally to the Lord.

Some churches have been very successful in their fundraising efforts. They have carwashes and bake sales, raffles and picnics, yard sales and bingos. Some even rent out their facilities to various clubs during the week to raise extra money. Such tactics, however, are without divine approval. The church is to be supported by the freewill offering of saints upon the first day of the week.

(5) **Praying.** The church is to be a praying-people. It is a privilege that Christians should take advantage of often (Lk. 18:1; Eph. 6:18; 1 Thess. 5:17).

It is impressive to see how much the early church prayed together. The Bible says they "continued steadfastly in the apostles' doctrine and fellowship, and in breaking of bread, and in prayers" (Acts 2:42). When Peter was cast into prison, we read that "prayer was made without ceasing of the church unto God for him" (Acts 12:5). Then later when Paul and his companions visited with the church in Tyre, the brethren "kneeled down on the shore, and prayed" (Acts 21:5). Indeed, the early church was a praying church. They were in constant communication with their Heavenly Father.

How to Pray

When the disciples asked about prayer, Jesus responded by giving them an outline (or model) to follow when praying. He said, "When ye pray, say, Our Father which art in heaven, Hallowed be thy name. Thy kingdom come. They will be done, as in heaven, so in earth. Give us day by day our daily bread. And forgive us our sins; for we forgive every one that is indebted to us. And lead us not into temptation; but deliver us from evil" (Lk. 11:2-4). Notice that they were told to address the Father in prayer, offer praises to His name, and make petitions for the kingdom, physical needs, forgiveness of sins, and deliverance from evil. Disciples are instructed to pray for other things as well. For instance, we should pray for those in authority (1 Tim. 2:1-2), for those who persecute us (Matt. 5:44), for the sick (Jam. 5:13-15), for boldness in preaching the gospel (Acts 4:29), and for open doors (Col. 4:3).

There is no particular place or posture required for praying. Jesus prayed in the mountains (Mk. 6:46), in the wilderness (Lk. 5:16), in the garden (Matt. 26:39), and even on the cross (Lk. 23:34, 46). Biblical characters prayed standing (Neh. 9:5), kneeling (Ezra 9:5), sitting (1 Chron. 17:16-27), and bowing (Ex. 34:8).

I find it interesting that prayer was always a part of the big moments in the Lord's life. Jesus prayed at His baptism, before choosing His apostles, at the transfiguration, in the garden of Gethsemane, and on the cross. The same should be true of His disciples. We should pray always, especially before making important decisions or doing important things.

Our prayers must be offered according to God's will. John declared, "And this is the confidence that we have in him, that, if we ask any thing according to his will, he heareth us" (1 Jn. 5:14). James made a similar point in his epistle when he wrote, "Ye ask, and receive not, because ye ask amiss, that ye may consume it upon your lusts" (Jam. 4:3). Notice that in order to receive in prayer, we must make sure that it is in accordance with divine revelation. This, I believe, is what it means to pray in the Spirit (Eph. 6:18; Jude 20).

Character Factor

The character of the one praying must be consistent with his profession of faith. A man cannot persist in sin and expect his petitions to be granted by God (1 Pet. 3:7). He must be obedient (1 Jn. 3:22), forgiving (Matt. 6:14-15), and righteous (Jam. 5:16). Peter wrote, "For the eyes of the Lord are over the righteous, and his ears are open unto their prayers: but the face of the Lord is against them that do evil" (1 Pet. 3:12). Furthermore, the one praying should have a humble spirit (1 Pet. 5:5). An arrogant, egotistic, puffed up brother who walks around "strutting his stuff" should not expect to have his prayers answered. Consider the parable of the Pharisee and publican. Jesus said, "Two men went up into the temple to pray; the one a Pharisee, and the other a publican. The Pharisee stood and prayed thus within himself, God, I thank thee, that I am not as other men are, extortioners, unjust, adulterers, or even as this publican. I fast twice in the week, I give tithes of all that I possess. And the publican, standing afar off, would not lift up so much as his eyes unto heaven, but smote upon his breast, saying, God be merciful to me a sinner. I tell you, this man went down to his house justified rather than the other: for every one that exalteth himself shall be abased; and he that humbleth himself shall be exalted" (Lk. 18:10-14). Humility is an absolutely essential ingredient for prayer.

Vain Prayers

Prayer must come from the heart. It should be meaningful and deliberate. Vain prayers are not acceptable to God. In the Sermon on the Mount, Jesus said, "But when ye pray, use not vain repetitions, as the heathen do: for they think that they shall be heard for their much speaking" (Matt. 6:7). Prayer is not to be a series of empty lines that are repeated over and over again without any real thought.

Christians should pray with earnest and sincere devotion at all times. "Use not vain repetitions."

Respect the Pattern

There have been numerous attacks made against the ancient order of worship. In many cases the doctrines of men have usurped the doctrines of Christ. True disciples, however, will reject such changes and do their best to imitate the early church pattern for worship. They will assemble together upon the first day of the week to (1) sing praises, (2) hear the gospel preached, (3) partake of the Lord's Supper, (4) give as they have prospered, and (5) pray to God.

Conduct in Worship

We must conduct ourselves properly in worship. It is to be done respectfully and reverently. When brethren chew gum, pass notes, whisper to one another, clip their fingernails, and sleep during the service, their worship is unworthy of Jesus Christ. We ought to come to the church building focused on what we are doing, having our hearts and minds prepared to pay homage to the great and wonderful God of heaven.

Conclusion

Man was created to worship God. Our primary purpose for existing is to glorify and serve Him. However, God will not accept vain worship (Matt. 15:9), ignorant worship (Acts 17:23), or will worship (Col. 2:23). Our worship must be according to the pattern revealed in the New Testament to be accepted. If the early church did not do it in their worship, neither should we!

Questions on Lesson 6

1. What is the purpose of the Lord's Supper?

2. What are the two elements of the Lord's Supper and what do they represent?

3. When is the Lord's Supper to be observed?

4. Where is the Lord's Supper to be observed?

5. How do we know the Lord's Supper was not to be a common meal?

6. Are Christians to tithe? Explain.

7. What should be our attitude in giving?

8. What sort of things are Christians to pray for?

9. Prayers are to be offered according to whose will?

10. What does it mean to use "vain repetitions"?

11. What should characterize our conduct in worship?

56 | The Simple Truth

Lesson 7

Organization of the Church

The New Testament speaks of the church in two senses — universal and local. The universal church consists of all the saved (Matt. 16:18; Eph. 3:10). It has no organization except Christ as the head, heaven as the headquarters. The local church consists of the saved who work and worship together in a particular locality (1 Cor. 1:2; 1 Thess. 1:1). It does have a specific organization as revealed in the New Testament.

God's arrangement for the local church is summed up in the first verse of the book to the Philippians. The Bible says, "Paul and Timothy, the servants of Jesus Christ, to all the saints in Christ Jesus which are at Philippi, with the bishops and deacons" (Phil. 1:1). Notice that the church had bishops (elders), deacons, and saints. That is the proper organizational structure of the local congregation.

It is important for us to understand that local churches are autonomous in nature. They are self-governing. They do not answer or report to any councils, synods, general assemblies, boards, or delegates. Nor do they report to other churches. Local churches act independently of one another, and have the right and ability to govern their own affairs.

(1) **Elders.** Each congregation is to be overseen by elders (Acts 20:28; 1 Pet. 5:2). They, as leaders, are responsible for the members and the work that is conducted.

A study of the New Testament reveals that local congregations in the first century had a plurality of elders. For instance, the church at Jerusalem had elders (Acts 15:4), the church at Ephesus had elders (Acts 20:17), and the church at Philippi had elders (Phil. 1:1). The churches in Lystra, Iconium, and Antioch had elders as well (Acts 14:21-23). The divine pattern is "elders in every church...in every city" (Acts 14:23; Tit. 1:5). We do not read about one man acting as "the pastor" over a congregation or one man acting as "the bishop" over a diocese in scripture.

The terms elder, presbyter, overseer, bishop, pastor, and shepherd all refer to the same group of men. They are used interchangeably. Consider the following two passages.

> **Acts 20:17, 28** — "And from Miletus he sent to Ephesus, and called the elders (presbyters) of the church...Take heed therefore unto yourselves, and to all the flock, over the which the Holy Ghost hath made you overseers (bishops) to feed (pastor, shepherd) the church of God, which he hath purchased with his own blood."

> **1 Pet. 5:1-2** — "The elders (presbyters) which are among you I exhort, who am also an elder (presbyter), and a witness of the sufferings of Christ, and also a partaker of the glory that shall be revealed: Feed (pastor, shepherd) the flock of God which is among you, taking the oversight (bishop) thereof, not by constraint, but willingly; not for filthy lucre, but of a ready mind."

As you can see, the terms elder, presbyter, overseer, bishop, pastor, and shepherd all refer to the same group of men, in the same way that the terms preacher and evangelist or police officer and cop do.

Work of Elders

Elders assume an awesome responsibility. They are in charge of overseeing the congregation. Paul, in his farewell address to the elders at Ephesus, said, "Take heed therefore unto yourselves, and to all the flock, over the which the Holy Ghost hath made you overseers, to feed the church of God, which he hath purchased with his own blood" (Acts 20:28). To "oversee" means to superintend or to look over. Elders need to vigilantly oversee all aspects of the church (1 Pet. 5:2). They should monitor the singing, the communion, the giving, the preaching, and the praying. They should inspect all the tracts and workbooks that are distributed as well. After all, elders will be held accountable for these things on the last day (Heb. 13:17).

The oversight of elders is limited to the local church (1 Pet. 5:2). They are not to manage the affairs of multiple congregations. In other words, elders at congregation A have no business dictating the decision making of congregation B.

Pastors

Many people in the world today see the preacher as the "pastor." They have been taught that he is the one who oversees the congregation. Such is not the case. Preachers and pastors (elders) have different responsibilities in the church.

> **Paul to elders:** "Take heed unto yourselves, and to all the flock" (Acts 20:28).

> **Paul to preacher:** "Take heed unto yourself, and to the doctrine" (1 Tim. 4:16).

Notice that the elders are told to tend to the flock, while the preacher is told to tend to the doctrine. That is how faithful churches of Christ are to function. The elders are to shepherd, while the preacher studies and proclaims the message.

Elders must set a good example for the sheep to follow. Peter wrote that elders are not to lord over the congregation, but are to be "examples to the flock" (1 Pet. 5:3). Elders should be dedicated husbands, committed fathers, honest businessmen, loving neighbors, upright citizens, and loyal servants of Jesus Christ. They should be men of integrity and sincerity. Elders must have a good report of people within the church as well as those without (1 Tim. 3:7). Can you imagine the reputation a congregation would have if one of her leaders were a known cheat or liar in the secular world? Her influence would be severely wounded. The flock and the community should see a Christ-like example in the leaders of the church.

Not only do the elders have a responsibility to the flock, but the flock has a responsibility to the elders. Paul wrote, "And we beseech you, brethren, to know them which labor among you, and are over you in the Lord, and admonish you; And to esteem them very highly in love for their work's sake. And be at peace among yourselves" (1 Thess. 5:12-13). The writer of Hebrews added, "Obey them that have the rule over you, and submit yourselves: for they watch for your souls, as they that must give account, that they may do it with joy, and not with grief: for that is unprofitable for you" (Heb. 13:17). Notice that the members of the congregation are told to know the elders, esteem them very highly for their work's sake, obey them, and submit to them. The only exception to these commands is when elders engage in sinful activity. "Elders are human beings and subject to error in teaching and conduct. What happens when this unfortunately occurs? Can nothing be done to correct the matter? When a Christian, including the evangelist, knows of such a condition he must stand for the right, trying to correct the elder and seeking for

60 | The Simple Truth

whatever disciplinary action is essential to the purity of the congregation...To fail to take action would be rebellion against God" (*God's Shepherds*, Robert C. Welch, pp. 61, 62). Ungodly elders must be held accountable for their conduct (1 Tim. 5:20).

Elders are not tyrants or dictators. They do not drive the sheep; they go before them. Some believe that Diotrephes was an elder in the church (3 Jn. 9). If so, he is a perfect example of what elders are not to be. Arrogant, controlling, domineering, egotistic, haughty, power-hungry, self-serving men should not be appointed as elders. Men who seek to "take over" and "run the church" will only cause problems in a leadership position. Godly elders will have a servant's heart, not a dictator's mentality. Below are some different translations of 1 Peter 5:3a.

> KJV — "Neither as being lords over God's heritage"
> RSV — "Not as domineering over those in your charge"
> NEB — "Not tyrannizing over those who are allotted to your care"
> NCV — "Do not be like a ruler over people you are responsible for"
> CEV — "Don't be bossy to those people who are in your care"
> Phillips — "You should aim not at being 'little tin gods'"
> Amplified — "Not (as arrogant, dictatorial and overbearing persons)
>   domineering over those in your charge"

Elders must be spiritually minded, recognizing that the church is unlike any other institution on earth. They need to appreciate the importance of truth and the value of souls.

Not A Title

It has become commonplace to see men refer to themselves as "Pastor Bill" or "Bishop Tom" or "Elder Jim." However, such terms are not to be worn as a religious title. They are simply designations. For instance, Peter referred to himself as simply "an elder" (1 Pet. 5:1), not as "Elder Peter." Jesus condemned the wearing of religious titles (Matt. 23:1-12).

Qualifications for Elders

Below are the qualifications for an elder listed in 1 Timothy 3 and Titus 1 of the King James Version. I have added my personal commentary in parenthesis.

1 Timothy 3

This is a true saying, If a man (though some versions translate this term as "anyone" or "someone," the context clearly reveals that it has reference to a male. No woman can be a husband or a father, nor can she scripturally rule the house) **desire the office of a bishop, he desireth a good work** (a man should not be forced into the office against his wishes. He should sincerely want to be an elder). **A bishop then must be blameless** (one against whom no evil charge can be sustained, above reproach), **the husband of one wife** (a man must have no more or less than one wife. This qualification denies unmarried men and polygamists from being elders. Some dispute has occurred over whether or not a man who has scripturally divorced his wife and married another meets this qualification. The answer is yes. Such a man has but one wife in the sight of God), **vigilant** (alert, watchful), **sober** (of a sound mind, sensible), **of good behavior** (orderly, well-behaved), **given to hospitality** (generous to guests), **apt to teach** (capable of teaching. An elder must have a sufficient knowledge of the truth so he can instruct and refute when necessary); **not given to wine** (not subject to wine or other intoxicating liquors), **no striker** (not violent), **not greedy of filthy lucre** (not greedy, not consumed with worldly wealth); **but patient** (forbearing, mild), **not a brawler** (not contentious or quarrelsome), **not covetous** (not a lover of money); **One that ruleth well his own house** (an elder must be able to control and manage his family in a respectable manner), **having his children in subjection with all gravity** (his children must be obedient, subordinate. Some dispute has occurred over whether or not a man with one child meets this qualification. The answer is yes. The terms "children" and "child" are used interchangeably in scripture (Gen. 21:7-8). Furthermore, no one seems to disagree that "children" would include one child in 1 Timothy 5:4, 10. Why the difference here? A man with one child should not be excluded from the office of elder if his child was raised in a godly manner. If we cannot say that he is without children, we must say he has children); **for if a man know not how to rule his own house, how shall he take care of the church of God?** (if a man is not capable of controlling his household, he cannot control the church. Men who allow their wives or children to "rule the roost" are not qualified to be elders) **Not a novice** (not a recent convert, not a babe in Christ), **lest being lifted up with pride he fall into the condemnation of the devil** (a man with little experience or spiritual maturity can quickly become puffed up in a role of authority). **Moreover he must have a good report of them which are without** (good reputation among unbelievers, known as a man of honesty and integrity in the world); **lest he fall into reproach and the snare of the devil** (an ungodly man who is carnally minded — corrupt in his speech, immodest in his

62 | The Simple Truth

dress, dishonest in his business affairs — will bring reproach upon himself and the church).

Titus 1

If any be blameless (one against whom no evil charge can be sustained, above reproach), **the husband of one wife** (a man must have no more or less than one wife. This qualification denies unmarried men and polygamists from being elders), **having faithful children** (his children must be Christians — "having children that believe" (ASV), "whose children are believers" (RSV), "their children must love the Lord" (LB), "their children must be followers of the Lord" (CEV). Perhaps the New Life Version (NLV) says it best: "their children must be Christians." That is the meaning of this qualification. Some dispute has occurred over whether or not a man who has a child to become unfaithful after leaving the house is still qualified to be an elder. The answer is yes. Jesus, "the chief Shepherd" (1 Pet. 5:4), could not keep some of His own from leaving (Jn. 6:66). Would any dare say He is unqualified? Furthermore, God the Father has many children who become unfaithful. Does that make Him a poor father? If an elder has proven his ability to lead his children while they are under his roof, he is qualified to serve) **not accused of riot** (not wild) **or unruly** (not insubordinate or rebellious), **for a bishop must be blameless** (one against whom no evil charge can be sustained, above reproach), **as the steward of God** (servant who manages the affairs of God); **not self-willed** (not headstrong, not selfish), **not soon angry** (not irritable or quick tempered), **not given to wine** (not subject to wine or other intoxicating liquors), **no striker** (not violent), **not given to filthy lucre** (not greedy, not consumed with worldly wealth); **but a lover of hospitality** (generous to guests), **a lover of good men** (loving goodness), **sober** (of a sound mind, sensible), **just** (equal, fair, righteous), **holy** (devout, pious, saintly), **temperate** (self-controlled, self-disciplined); **holding fast the faithful word as he hath been taught, that he may be able by sound doctrine both to exhort and to convince the gainsayers** (elders must be grounded in the truth so they can exhort and convince when necessary).

Although we do not want to make the qualifications too difficult, it is vitally important to make sure that men are qualified before they are appointed as overseers. Paul told Timothy, "Lay hands suddenly on no man" (1 Tim. 5:22). This means that great thought and deliberation should occur before the appointment of elders. It is better to go without elders than to have unqualified elders in office.

(2) **Deacons.** Deacons tend to the physical needs of the congregation. For instance, in Acts 6 we read about a problem that occurred in the church at

Jerusalem. Some of the widows were being neglected in the daily distribution of food. Therefore, the congregation selected seven men to tend to their needs. The Bible says, "And in those days, when the number of disciples was multiplied, there arose a murmuring of the Grecians against the Hebrews, because their widows were neglected in the daily ministration. Then the twelve called the multitude of disciples unto them, and said, It is not reason that we should leave the word of God, and serve tables. Wherefore, brethren, look ye out among you seven man of honest report, full of the Holy Ghost and wisdom, whom we may appoint over this business. But we will give ourselves continually to prayer, and to the ministry of the word. And the saying pleased the whole multitude: and they chose Stephen, a man full of the Holy Ghost, and Philip, and Prochorus, and Nicanor, and Timon, and Parmenas, and Nicolas a proselyte of Antioch: Whom they set before the apostles: and when they had prayed, they laid their hands on them" (vv. 1-6). Notice that the seven men were not appointed to preach the gospel or to oversee the flock. They were appointed to "serve tables" (v. 2), meaning they made sure that the widows were fed properly. Although we do not know for sure if these seven men were officially deacons, we do know that they performed the work of deacons.

Elders should put deacons to work. Oftentimes deacons are appointed, but never do anything. They just sit in the pew stagnant. Deacons should be called upon to serve!

The qualifications for a deacon can be found in 1 Timothy 3:8-13. Deacons must be men of dignity and integrity. They, along with their wives, should conduct themselves in a manner that is worthy of respect by all.

The Preacher

There is no greater work under heaven than that of preaching the gospel. Paul wrote, "For whosoever shall call upon the name of the Lord shall be saved. How then shall they call on him in whom they have not believed? And how shall they believe in him of whom they have not heard? And how shall they hear without a preacher? And how shall they preach, except they be sent? As it is written, How beautiful are the feet of them that preach the gospel of peace, and bring glad tidings of good things" (Rom. 10:13-15). A man willing to dedicate his life to the proclamation of the truth should be commended and encouraged by all the saved.

Paul outlines the work of the preacher in his letters to Timothy and Titus. Below are some key passages to consider.

1 Timothy 4:6 — "If thou put the brethren in remembrance of these things, thou shalt be a good minister of Jesus Christ, nourished up in the words of faith and of good doctrine, whereunto thou hast attained."

1 Timothy 4:13 — "Till I come, give attendance to reading, to exhortation, to doctrine."

1 Timothy 4:16 — "Take heed unto thyself, and unto the doctrine; continue in them: for in doing this thou shalt both save thyself, and them that hear thee."

2 Timothy 2:2 — "And the things that thou hast heard of me among many witnesses, the same commit thou to faithful men, who shall be able to teach others also."

2 Timothy 2:15 — "Study to show thyself approved unto God, a workman that needeth not to be ashamed, rightly dividing the word of truth."

2 Timothy 4:2 — "Preach the word; be instant in season, out of season; reprove, rebuke, exhort with all longsuffering and doctrine."

Titus 2:1 — "But speak thou the things which become sound doctrine."

Notice that the preacher is to study the scriptures and inform others through preaching and teaching. It is not his responsibility to oversee the congregation or to serve tables. Furthermore, he is not the "church policeman" who sees to it that each member is living right. It is his duty to proclaim the laws of God, not to enforce them.

Some brethren see the preacher as the "church employee." They think he is paid to cut the grass, water the flowers, visit the sick, fix the furnace, paint the classrooms, and be an errand boy for the members. Such is not the case. He is no more responsible for those other things than any other member of the church. He is paid to preach!

Preachers Must Contend

Preachers must be men of conviction. As heralds of the truth they will face opposition from time to time. Therefore, they should stand ready always to defend the gospel (Phil. 1:17) and contend for the faith (Jude 3), remembering that truth does not fear investigation, it welcomes it. Compromisers have no business in the pulpit.

I recognize that the servant of the Lord must "be gentle unto all men" (2 Tim. 2:24). However, we must not confuse gentleness and softness. They are not the same. For instance, Paul, in 1 Thessalonians 2, said that he was gentle among them (v. 7), yet he was "bold" and spoke the gospel "with much contention" (v. 2).

When Paul gave his farewell address to the elders at Ephesus, he said, "I kept back nothing that was profitable unto you...Wherefore I take you to record this day, that I am pure from the blood of all men. For I have not shunned to declare unto you all the counsel of God" (Acts 20:20, 26-27). Such should be the aim of every gospel preacher. He must not hold back any part of the truth, nor allow friendships or other relationships to muzzle him from addressing certain issues within the congregation.

The preacher often receives more credit than he deserves when things are going well, and more criticism than he deserves when things are not going well. Doing the work of an evangelist is not an easy job. It is difficult. It is wearisome. Encourage your preacher, and let him know that he is appreciated and loved in the Lord for the work he does.

Women Preachers

There is no such thing as a second-class citizen in the kingdom. Men and women are equal in the sight of God (Gal. 3:28). However, God has given men and women different roles in the church. Men are to be the preachers in the assembly, not women. Paul wrote, "Let the woman learn in silence with all subjection. But I suffer not a woman to teach, nor to usurp authority over the man, but to be in silence" (1 Tim. 2:11-12). Notice that women are not to usurp authority over the man (i.e., exercise dominion over him). How then can women scripturally occupy the pulpit? They can't. This passage clearly forbids women from preaching in the assembly. Paul made a similar point in his letter to the Corinthians (1 Cor. 14:34-35).

Consider this: Preachers are told to speak with all authority (Tit. 2:15). Women are not to usurp authority over the man (1 Tim. 2:12). Therefore, women cannot be preachers in the assembly and be pleasing to God!

This is not to say that women have no place in teaching. They do. Paul instructed older women to teach the younger women (Tit. 2:3-5), Priscilla helped her husband in teaching a non-Christian (Acts 18:26), and Timothy, as a child, was taught by his mother (2 Tim. 1:5). Furthermore, all Christians, including women, teach in their singing (Col. 3:16). They simply cannot assume a position that would cause them to usurp authority over the man.

In 2 Chronicles 26, we read about King Uzziah. Early in his reign he sought the Lord and prospered exceedingly (v. 5). He prospered in war, in reputation, in development projects, and in military might. However, when he became lifted up with pride and tried to invade the priest's office, thus ignoring the roles God had revealed in His Word, he was plagued with leprosy and died. Can you not see the parallel to women preaching in the assembly? They are exhibiting the same rebellious attitude that Uzziah had. Just as he ignored what God said about who was to burn incense in the temple, they are ignoring what God says about who is to preach in the church. Let us learn from Uzziah!

Committees

Many churches have created committees to oversee certain aspects of the work. Such committees are unauthorized. For instance, where do we read about a finance committee, transportation committee, youth committee, visitation committee, advertising committee, preaching committee, or welcoming committee in the New Testament? We don't! The elders are to oversee the work, not various man-made committees. Furthermore, committees often eliminate all the other members from doing the work that all members are to do, such as visiting the sick and welcoming the visitors. The first century church did not have these various committees, and neither should we!

Conclusion

The organizational structure of the church is not a matter of personal opinion or private interpretation. It is a matter of faith. Congregations that are true and faithful will follow the arrangement revealed in the New Testament. We do not read about a pope, cardinal, archbishop, senior pastor, or church president in the scriptures. Every local church is to have elders, deacons, and saints (Phil. 1:1).

Questions on Lesson 7

1. In what two senses does the New Testament speak of the church? What is the difference?

2. What does it mean for churches to be autonomous?

3. What does the New Testament teach about the number of elders in each church?

4. Briefly describe the work of the elders.

5. Are elders and pastors different offices or the same? Explain.

6. Are the qualifications outlined in 1 Timothy 3 and Titus 1 required for elders, or are they optional? Explain.

7. Briefly describe the work of deacons.

8. Briefly describe the work of a preacher.

9. Are women authorized to preach in the assembly? Explain.

Lesson 8

Denominationalism

The Lord promised to build His church. He declared, "Upon this rock I will build my church; and the gates of hell shall not prevail against it" (Matt. 16:18). He purchased it with His own blood (Acts 20:28). The church of Christ came into existence on the day of Pentecost in Acts 2, in fulfillment of prophecy (Is. 2:2-4; Mic. 4:1-2).

Some argue that the church was established during the personal ministry of Christ. If that were true, it had no blood (Jn. 19:34), no head (Eph. 1:22-23), no completed gospel (1 Cor. 15:1-4), no redemption (Heb. 9:15, 22), and no new testament (Heb. 9:16-17). Who can believe such a thing? Not only that, but it would have existed under the limited commission and its members could not have gloried in the cross. Acts 2 is the first time the church is spoken of in the present tense.

Marks of Identification

If I were trying to find one particular child in a crowded classroom, what would I look for? I would look for marks of identification (brown hair, blue eyes, wearing red shirt). The same is true with finding the church of our Lord. We must look for identifying marks that will separate it from all the others.

Jesus Christ founded the church of the New Testament. It belongs to Him. Furthermore, the church was established in the city of Jerusalem, wore the name of Christ, and followed no creed but God's Word. These marks will reveal which church is the true church of our Lord today. Consider the following charts.

Church Name	Founder
Church of Christ	Jesus Christ
Catholic Church	Boniface III
Lutheran Church	Martin Luther
Presbyterian Church	John Calvin
Baptist Church	John Smyth
Methodist Church	John Wesley

Church Name	Date/Location
Church of Christ	30-33 AD / Jerusalem
Catholic Church	606-607 AD / Rome
Lutheran Church	1520-1530 AD / Germany
Presbyterian Church	1536 AD / Switzerland
Baptist Church	1607-1611 AD / Holland
Methodist Church	1739 AD / England

Church Name	Creed Book
Church of Christ	Bible
Catholic Church	Bible / Catholic Catechism
Lutheran Church	Bible / Augsburg Confession
Presbyterian Church	Bible / Confession of Faith
Baptist Church	Bible / Standard Manual
Methodist Church	Bible / Methodist Discipline

The "church of Christ" is the church of the New Testament. It is the one and only church that has all the marks of identification. Every other church was founded by the *wrong* person, at the *wrong* place, at the *wrong* time.

Why would anyone want to be a member of Martin Luther's church when they could belong to the Lord's church? Why would they want to be a "Lutheran" when they could be a "Christian?" That goes for all other man-made churches as well.

The church is the bride of Christ. What name should the bride of Christ wear? She should wear His name, the name of Christ, of course. That is why the early churches were referred to as "churches of Christ" (Rom. 16:16). There was no such thing as a "Baptist Church," "Presbyterian Church," "Methodist Church," "Episcopal Church," or "Lutheran Church" in the first century. Those unscriptural institutions and their names originated with men, not God. The New Testament knows but one church, and it wears the name of Christ.

Denominationalism

The New Testament speaks of the church in two senses — universal and local. Denominations do not qualify as either. Think about it. They are too small to be the universal church (all of the saved) and too big to be the local church (saved who worship together in a particular locality). Hence, denominationalism is not scriptural.

Many people fail to realize that denominationalism is a work of the devil that contradicts the prayer of our Lord (Jn. 17:20-23) and the plea of Paul (1 Cor. 1:10-13). It stands in direct opposition to God's divine pattern. Consider the following chart.

Denominationalism	God's Pattern
Different Churches	One Church
Different Creeds	One Creed
Different Heads	One Head
Different Baptisms	One Baptism
Different Rules	One Rule

From the above chart we can see that denominationalism stands in direct opposition to God's divine pattern. Therefore, we must preach and teach against denominationalism.

Consider some of the statements made by well-known religious leaders of the past about the wearing of denominational names. They are very telling.

Martin Luther: "I ask that men make no reference to my name, and call themselves not Lutherans, but Christians" (*A Compend of Luther's Theology*, p. 135).

John Wesley: "Would to God that all party names, and unscriptural phrases and forms which have divided the Christian world, were forgot" (*Universal Knowledge*, Vol. IX, p. 540).

Charles Spurgeon: "I look forward with pleasure to the day when there will not be a Baptist living! I hope that the Baptist name will soon perish, but let Christ's name last forever" (*Spurgeon Memorial Library*, Vol. I, p. 168).

Arguments Used to Justify Denominationalism

Below are four common arguments used to justify denominationalism. Please consider the argument and the answer that follows. Can denominationalism be sustained?

The "other sheep" in John 10:16 refer to denominations. The "other sheep" refer to the Gentiles, not to denominational churches. Jesus was stating that Gentiles would be saved and be given a place in the fold as well as Jews (Eph. 2:16). He still said there would be but "one fold."

The "branches" in John 15:1-6 refer to denominations. The "branches" refer to individuals, not to denominational churches. The context clearly reveals that Jesus was speaking of an individual's productivity or lack thereof. He said, "If a man abide not in me" not "if a denomination abide not in me" (v. 6).

The "seven churches" in Revelation 2-3 were different denominations. If the "seven churches" were different denominations, which ones were they? Was the church at Ephesus the Ephesus Episcopalian Church? Was the church at Pergamos the Pergamos Presbyterian Church? Was the church at Laodicea the Laodicea Lutheran Church? The very thought is absurd. These churches were not different denominations. They were simply local congregations of the same body. These churches all believed the same doctrines and practiced the same things. They were all "churches of Christ" (Rom. 16:16).

The incident in Mark 9:38-39 shows that people can belong to different denominations and still be acceptable to Jesus. The man who was casting out devils had been given authority from Jesus to do so. We know that to be true because of the miracles he was able to perform. The difference between this man and denominations is twofold: (1) He was an individual and (2) He had authority from Jesus.

None of the arguments listed above sustain denominationalism. There is no authority whatsoever for denominational churches to exist. "Except the Lord build the house, they labor in vain that build it" (Ps. 127:1).

Conclusion

Churches that were created by mere men are counterfeit churches. They are frauds. The Father only planned one church; the Son only purchased one church; the Spirit only revealed one church. It is the church of Christ. Let us reject all other religious bodies. "Every plant, which my Heavenly Father hath not planted, shall be rooted up" (Matt. 15:13).

Questions on Lesson 8

1. When did the Lord's church come into existence?

2. What identifying marks separate the Lord's church from other churches?

3. Since the church is the bride of Christ, what does that imply with regard to the name it wears?

4. How does denominationalism contradict God's pattern?

5. When Jesus spoke of Himself as "the true vine" (John 15:1-6), did He teach that the branches were individuals or denominations? Explain.

6. Were the seven churches in Revelation 2-3 different denominations? Explain.

Lesson 9

Falling from Grace

Can a child of God fall from grace? That question has been discussed and debated many times in various places. It has caused much dissension in the religious world. People have very strong convictions about the matter. However, our objective is to find the scriptural answer to the above question, disregarding all preconceived ideas and prejudices.

Faith. We all agree that faith is very important. The Bible says that without faith it is impossible to please God (Heb. 11:6). We are justified by faith (Rom. 5:1). Yet from Paul's first letter to Timothy we see that there are many horrific things that a child of God can do with his faith. Consider the chart below.

Shipwreck faith	1 Tim. 1:19
Depart from the faith	1 Tim. 4:1
Deny the faith	1 Tim. 5:8
Cast off the faith	1 Tim. 5:12
Err concerning the faith	1 Tim. 6:21

Surely no one believes that a child of God can have his faith shipwrecked, depart from the faith, deny the faith, cast off the faith, and err concerning the faith — and still be saved! Yet Paul acknowledged that a Christian could do all of those things.

Hebrews. The Hebrew brethren were members of the early church. They were called "holy brethren, partakers of the heavenly calling" (Heb. 3:1). There can be no doubt that the writer of the book was in fellowship with those Christians. Yet we see that there were many horrific things that they could do. Consider the chart below.

Depart from God	Heb. 3:12
Be hardened through deceit of sin	Heb. 3:13
Come short of the promise	Heb. 4:1
Fall after example of unbelief	Heb. 4:11
Count the blood unholy	Heb. 10:29
Cast away confidence	Heb. 10:35
Fail of the grace of God	Heb. 12:15
Refuse him from heaven	Heb. 12:25
Be carried by strange doctrines	Heb. 13:9

Surely no one believes that a child of God can depart from God, be hardened through the deceitfulness of sin, come short of the promise, fall after the example of unbelief, count the blood unholy, cast away his confidence, fail of the grace of God, refuse Him that speaks from heaven, and be carried about by strange doctrines — and still be saved! Yet the Hebrews writer acknowledged that a Christian could do all of those things.

This is not to say that a child of God has no assurance or confidence. We all believe that he has assurance. In fact, Jesus promised that the believer "shall not come into condemnation" (Jn. 5:24). However, we must understand that a believer can become an unbeliever. He can develop "an evil heart of unbelief in departing from the living God" (Heb. 3:12). The blessed assurance of "no condemnation" is promised only to those who "walk not after the flesh, but after the Spirit" (Rom. 8:1). As long as a child of God walks after the Spirit he can have absolute assurance in his salvation!

If. The word "if" is a little word with a big meaning. It is a conditional word. If a father tells his son, "I will take you to the movies if you clean your room," we all recognize that the son must meet a condition before going to the movies — he must clean his room. The same is true with our salvation from sin. There are conditions we must meet and maintain. Consider the chart below.

Disciples	IF ye continue in my word (Jn. 8:31)
Honored	IF a man serve me (Jn. 12:26)
Saved	IF ye keep in memory (1 Cor. 15:1-2)
Reap	IF we faint not (Gal. 6:9)
Holy	IF we continue in the faith (Col. 1:23)
Never Fall	IF ye do these things (2 Pet. 1:10)
Cleansed	IF ye walk in the light (1 Jn. 1:7)

Every honest person can see that there are conditions that a child of God must meet and maintain to be saved. Even the most stubborn soul must concede that "if" is a conditional word.

Examples. We could look at examples of actual people who fell away in the New Testament. Hymeneus, Alexander, Philetus, and Demas are all identified as having fallen from grace (1 Tim. 1:19-20; 2 Tim. 2:17; 4:10). Ananias and Sapphira were members of the church at Jerusalem who were struck dead for lying to the Holy Ghost (Acts 5:1-10). What about Simon? He was a child of God who was told to repent of his wickedness, that he may be forgiven (Acts 8:22). Would he be saved if he refused to repent? Of course not. These names are etched in history as a vivid reminder that a child of God can forfeit his salvation. He can "depart from the faith" (1 Tim. 4:1).

Advocates of the "once saved — always saved" doctrine argue that a person who falls away never really believed in the first place. They say he was only a pretender. However, Jesus made a statement that destroys this argument. In the parable of the sower, He said, "They on the rock are they, which, when they hear, receive the word with joy; and these have no root, which for a while believe, and in time of temptation fall away" (Lk. 8:13). Notice that they believed and then fell away. No one can say that they did not really believe, for Jesus said they did! Hence, this argument is proven erroneous. Furthermore, the Israelites are another example of believers who fell away. The Bible says, "And the people feared the Lord, and believed the Lord, and his servant Moses" (Ex. 14:31). Yet thousands of them later fell (1 Cor. 10:8). Do not be deceived by such arguments.

78 | The Simple Truth

Fall. Probably the most obvious way to determine if a child of God can fall from grace is to look at the word "fall" in scripture. Is it there? How is it used? What does it teach? Consider the chart below.

In time of temptation fell away (Lk. 8:13)
Take heed lest ye fall (1 Cor. 10:12)
Ye are fallen from grace (Gal. 5:4)
Lest ye fall into temptation (Jam. 5:12)
Lest ye fall from your own steadfastness (2 Pet. 3:17)
Remember from whence thou art fallen (Rev. 2:5)

The fact that the word "fall" is used in reference to Christians settles the issue. Our objective was to determine "Can a child of God fall from grace?" The Bible says yes, a child of God can fall!

Questions. A child of God can lie (Col. 3:9). What if he lies, but never repents? Will he still be saved? The Bible says that all liars shall have their part in the lake which burneth with fire and brimstone (Rev. 21:8). A child of God can also get drunk (Eph. 5:18). What if he gets drunk, but never repents? Will he still be saved? The Bible says that drunkards will not inherit the kingdom of heaven (1 Cor. 6:9-10). Furthermore, a child of God who refuses to provide for his house "hath denied the faith, and is worse than an infidel" (1 Tim. 5:8). Will he still be saved? These are appropriate questions that need to be answered.

Peter, in graphic detail, describes the pitiful condition of those who fall from grace. He wrote, "For if after they have escaped the pollutions of the world through the knowledge of the Lord and Savior Jesus Christ, they are again entangled therein, and overcome, the latter end is worse with them than the beginning. For it had been better for them not to have known the way of righteousness, than, after they have known it, to turn from the holy commandment delivered unto them. But it is happened unto them according to the true proverb, The dog is turned to his own vomit again; and the sow that was washed to her wallowing in the mire" (2 Pet. 2:20-22). How sad.

The "once saved — always saved" doctrine is false. Christians must remain faithful to stay in favor with God and to receive a crown of life (Rev. 2:10). Here is one final chart to consider.

Saved by:	But Can:
Faith	Depart from faith (1 Tim. 4:1)
Gospel	Believe gospel in vain (1 Cor. 15:2)
God	Depart from God (Heb. 3:12)
Lord	Deny the Lord (2 Pet. 2:1)
Truth	Err from the truth (Jam. 5:19)
Blood	Count blood unholy (Heb. 10:29)
Grace	Fail of the grace (Heb. 12:15)

Questions on Lesson 9

1. What did Paul tell Timothy that a child of God could do with his faith?

2. What did the Hebrew writer say that Christians could do to forfeit their salvation?

3. If a Christian can fall from grace, can he still be confident in his salvation? Explain.

80 | The Simple Truth

4. What two-letter word found in the Bible shows us that salvation by grace is conditional?

5. Some who believe the "once saved, always saved" doctrine will argue that one who falls away never believed in the first place. Explain why this concept is false.

6. What did Peter say about the state of those who once were saved, but later fell from grace (2 Peter 2:20-22)?

Lesson 10

Wearing Religious Titles

It has become commonplace for preachers to wear religious titles. They are called "Reverend," "Father," "Doctor," "Cardinal," "Presiding Bishop," and many other such things. Therefore, this chapter will examine the issue of wearing religious titles.

Jesus condemned the wearing of religious titles in Matthew 23. He said, "But be not ye called Rabbi: for one is your Master, even Christ; and all ye are brethren. And call no man your father upon the earth: for one is your Father, which is in heaven. Neither be ye called masters: for one is your Master, even Christ" (vv. 8-10). Notice that the Lord did not want His disciples wearing religious titles. They were simply to be called "brethren" (v. 8).

Some people have a hard time reconciling the statement "call no man your father" with other passages that use the term father in the New Testament (Acts 16:1; 1 Thess. 2:11; 1 Tim. 5:1; etc). The difference is clear. Jesus was condemning the wearing of religious titles, not the secular use of the word. For instance, suppose someone said, "Douglas Erhardt is Aaron's father." In that context the word father would be acceptable because it is not used as a religious title. On the other hand, however, suppose someone said, "My spiritual advisor is Father Bill Davis." In that context it would be wrong because it is used as a religious title.

I grew up in Roman Catholicism. During that time I was taught to call the parish priest "Father." Now looking back I ask myself, "How could they do the very thing that Jesus said not to do?" Whereas Jesus said, "Call no man your father" in a religious sense, they demand that it be done!

First Century Preachers

It is important to note that not one gospel preacher in the early church wore a religious title. Not one. We must look outside the New Testament to find such practices. For instance, consider Paul and Timothy. They were two of the most influential preachers to ever live. Surely then they would be addressed with some glamorous and glowing title, right? Wrong. Peter simply addressed Paul as "our beloved brother Paul" (2 Pet. 3:15), and the Hebrews writer addressed Timothy as "our brother Timothy" (Heb. 13:23). They were never called "Reverend," "Father," or "Doctor." In fact, two letters were written to Timothy and one to the evangelist Titus in the New Testament. None of the greetings included a religious title. They were just called "Timothy" and "Titus." The same could be said about Philip, Apollos, Archippus, and every other evangelist of that time.

Preachers in the early church did not want to be elevated or exalted above their brethren in any way. They did not wear robes or titles. Preachers today ought to follow their humble example.

Reverend

The Psalmist declared of God, "He sent redemption unto his people; he hath commanded his covenant forever: holy and reverend is his name" (Ps. 111:9). Notice that "holy and reverend" is God's name. He is the One to be feared and honored. Why then do so many men want to assume that designation for themselves? Why do they insist that others call them "Reverend?" Could it be that such men have swelled up with pride and caught a case of "Phariseeitis," meaning, "all their works they do to be seen of men" (Matt. 23:5)? Holy and reverend is God's name, not a denominational preacher's name! Consider the following quote taken from a book written by a Baptist historian.

> "The term *Reverend*, now in such common use among our people and all other parties, was generally very offensive to Baptists of the old school, and was seldom employed by them in common conversation, in letter inscriptions, or in any other way. *Holy and reverend is his name*, as a designation of the Divine Being, was a passage often quoted by objectors to giving reverence to men. To the Deity alone, said they, reverence belongs" (*50 Years Among the Baptists*, David Benedict, p. 286).

Humility Factor

All Christians should be people of humility (Jam. 4:6). They should seek to esteem others above themselves (Phil. 2:3). How then can preachers insist that men call them by special titles of exaltation such as "Father" or "Reverend" and still display humility? They can't. Humility would refuse men's praise, not accept it (Acts 10:25-26; 14:14-15).

I have a beloved brother in the Lord who has received PhD's in both the Hebrew and Greek language. He has been asked to teach classes at prestigious universities all across the country. Yet most of our brethren have no idea that it is so. That is because he is a man of humility who is concerned with glorifying Christ, not himself. He never signs his name with a "PhD" at the end or introduces himself as such. That is the same attitude preachers in the early church had.

Conclusion

Jesus condemned the wearing of religious titles in Matthew 23. There is no evidence whatsoever that preachers in the early church wore such titles. Therefore, we should not wear them either. Let us reject and resist these things. *To God be the glory!*

Questions on Lesson 10

1. What are some religious titles that men wear today?

2. What did Jesus say about wearing such religious titles?

3. How were preachers referred to in the New Testament?

4. According to the scriptures, who is "reverend"?

5. What essential characteristic would prevent one from wearing a religious title?

Lesson 11

The Kingdom

Premillennialists teach that the kingdom is not currently in existence. They say that although Christ intended to set up the kingdom while on earth the first time, He was crucified before He could do it. Are they correct? Let us investigate.

Kingdom in Prophecy

In Daniel 2, King Nebuchadnezzar had a dream that troubled him. When the wise men of the nation could not interpret the dream he ordered them to be slain. Daniel, however, a prophet of God, volunteered to interpret it. He said, "Thou, O king, sawest, and behold a great image. This great image, whose brightness was excellent, stood before thee; and the form thereof was terrible" (v. 31). He then went on to describe the image and what it represented.

The sections of the image represented four consecutive world-ruling empires. The first was Babylonia (626-539), then Medo-Persia (539-330), then Greece (330-63), and finally Rome (63+). Daniel then declared, "And in the days of these kings shall the God of heaven set up a kingdom, which shall never be destroyed: and the kingdom will not be left to other people, but it shall break in pieces and consume all these kingdoms, and it shall stand forever" (v. 44). Hence, the kingdom would be established during the Roman Empire's rule.

In Daniel 7, we are told that the kingdom would be given to the Lord when going to the Ancient of days in heaven (vv. 13-14). Obviously that refers to the time of the ascension. "There should be no argument as to who or what this scene referred. Daniel spoke from heaven's point of view. He was describing the return of God's Son, as the Son of man and the Son of God, when He received the promised kingdom from His Father. And Luke, speaking from earth's point of view, described the same event in the first two chapters of Acts" (*A Commentary on Daniel*, Homer Hailey, p. 140).

Kingdom in Promise

When we reach the gospel accounts, Rome was the world-ruling empire. It was time for Daniel's prophecy to be fulfilled. It is no wonder then that John the Baptist and Jesus declared that the kingdom was "at hand" (Matt. 3:2; Mk. 1:15). In fact, Jesus promised that it would be established during that generation. He said, "Verily I say unto you, That there be some of them that stand here, which shall not taste of death, till they have seen the kingdom of God come with power" (Mk. 9:1). Thus, the stage was set for the ushering in of the kingdom.

Kingdom in Fulfillment

The kingdom was indeed established in the first century. There are many passages that prove this point. Consider the following.

> **Colossians 1:13** — "Who hath delivered us from the power of darkness, and hath translated us into the kingdom of his dear Son."

> **1 Thessalonians 2:12** — "That ye walk worthy of God, who hath called you unto his kingdom and glory."

> **Hebrews 12:28** — "Wherefore we receiving a kingdom which cannot be moved, let us have grace, whereby we may serve God acceptably with reverence and godly fear."

> **Revelation 1:9** — "I John, who also am your brother, and companion in tribulation, and in the kingdom and patience of Jesus Christ, was in the isle that is called Patmos, for the word of God, and for the testimony of Jesus Christ."

Notice that the Colossian brethren were in the kingdom, the Thessalonian brethren were in the kingdom, the Hebrew brethren were in the kingdom, and John the apostle was in the kingdom. How then can anyone teach that the kingdom is not currently in existence?

Consider this: Revelation 1:6 states that Christ "made us to be a kingdom and priests" (NIV). How could that be if Premillennialism were true? It couldn't be.

We must understand that the kingdom is spiritual in nature (Lk. 17:20-21). It was never intended to be an earthly kingdom, bound by geographical boundaries. It is "not of this world" (Jn. 18:36).

Harmful Consequences

There are many harmful consequences for those who deny that the kingdom is in existence. For instance, if there is no kingdom, no one has been converted (Matt. 18:3), no one has been born again (Jn. 3:5), no one has a right to eat the Lord's Supper (Lk. 22:18), and no one has been delivered from the power of darkness (Col. 1:13).

Premillennialism makes Jesus a failure the first time. Think about it. To say that He intended to set up the kingdom, but was stopped from doing it, makes Him unsuccessful the first time. It makes Him a failure. Who can believe such nonsense? Premillennialism also makes Him a King without a kingdom. I am convinced that many who have embraced this doctrine did so based solely on emotion, without consulting the scriptures. I pray they will reconsider their belief. To deny the kingdom's existence is to deny the truth of God's Word!

Kingdom & Church

In many instances, the terms "kingdom" and "church" are used interchangeably in scripture. They refer to the same institution (Matt. 16:18-19). They share the same origin in date and place, the same territory, the same ownership, and the same requirements for membership. Furthermore, the Lord's Supper is said to be in both the kingdom (Lk. 22:18) and the church (1 Cor. 11). Premillennialists err when they try to separate the two.

Misapplying Revelation

Premillennialists argue that their doctrine can be sustained in the book of Revelation. However, such is not the case. The book of Revelation was written in signs and symbols (1:1), meaning that much of it is figurative language. It pertained to things "which must shortly be done" (22:6). It was not written about activities and events that would transpire just before the Second Coming!

Revelation 20:4 is one of the most frequently used passages by Premillennialists to teach that Jesus will come back to earth, set up a kingdom, and reign for a thousand years. Is that what the passage says? Please note that the passage says nothing about Jerusalem, the Second Coming, Christ stepping foot on the earth, a bodily resurrection, the literal throne of David, or even us. The passage is talking about martyrs! All of those key components of their doctrine must be added (Rev. 22:18).

Conclusion

Premillennialists are wrong. The kingdom was established in the first century as prophesied and promised. It is a spiritual kingdom that will stand forever. Are you a citizen in the kingdom of God?

Questions on Lesson 11

1. What do Premillennialists teach about the kingdom?

2. What are the four world empires represented in Nebuchadnezzar's dream in Daniel 2?

3. What does Nebuchadnezzar's dream tell us about when the kingdom would be established?

4. What did Jesus say about the timing of His kingdom's establishment in Mark 9:1?

5. Where were the Colossians in relation to the kingdom (Colossians 1:13)?

6. How can we know that the kingdom is the church?

7. How do we know that Revelation 20:4 is not referring to a future 1,000-year reign of Christ on the earth as the Premillennialists contend?

90 | The Simple Truth

Lesson 12

Quick Tips for Study

Christians are commanded to study God's Word. This is a trait that is lacking today among the disciples. What ever happened to the time when members of the church of Christ were known as "Bible toting — scripture quoting" people? What ever happened to the time when we were respected for our knowledge of the holy book? I pray for a return to those days. It can only happen if we get back to studying.

The Bible says, "Study to show thyself approved unto God, a workman that needeth not to be ashamed, rightly dividing the word of truth" (2 Tim. 2:15). We should constantly meditate upon the scriptures, knowing that a lack of knowledge leads to destruction (Is. 5:13; Hos. 4:6). Below are eight quick tips for studying God's Word.

(1) **Read with confidence.** Realize that the Bible was written in a way that can be understood by the common man (Eph. 3:4; 5:17; 1 Tim. 2:4). Can you imagine how cruel and unjust God would be if He judged us based on something that could not be known? You do not need a college education or clergyman to know the truth (Jn. 8:32).

(2) **Discern the different covenants.** The old covenant was temporary, and has been done away with (Jer. 31:31; Col. 2:14). We are not under the authority of the Mosaic Law today. Our authority must come from the new covenant alone (Rom. 10:4; Gal. 3:23-25). Consider the chart below.

Old Law		New Law
Kills	2 Cor. 3:6	Gives Life
Condemnation	2 Cor. 3:9	Righteousness
Bondage	Gal. 5:1	Liberty
Shadow	Col. 2:17	Body
By Prophets	Heb. 1:1-2	By Christ
Faulty	Heb. 8:6-7	Excellent
Taken Away	Heb. 10:9	Established

Surely you can see that the new covenant is superior to the old covenant. It is the perfect standard that will judge us in the last day (Jn. 12:48; Jam. 2:12).

(3) **Consider the historical context in which it was written.** When Jesus said, "But pray that your flight be not in the winter, neither on the Sabbath day" (Matt. 24:20), He was talking about the destruction of Jerusalem in A.D. 70. It applied specifically to that generation (Matt. 24:34). To properly understand the gospel, we must consider the historical contexts and/or settings.

(4) **Keep the passage in context.** When Jesus was being tempted, the devil used scripture to entice Him to sin (Matt. 4:6). However, the scripture was taken out of context. Make sure scripture is not being misapplied.

(5) **Notice to whom the command was given.** Some commands apply to all people, while others are given specifically to an individual or group. For instance, when God said, "Make thee an ark of gopher wood" (Gen. 6:14), He was talking specifically to Noah, not to you and me. The same is true when God said, "Take now thy son...and offer him there for a burnt offering" (Gen. 22:2). That command was given specifically to Abraham. Furthermore, when Peter said, "Repent...and pray God if perhaps the thought of thine heart may be forgiven thee" (Acts 8:22), he was talking to an erring Christian. That command had no reference or relevance at all to an alien sinner. Alien sinners must "Repent, and be baptized...for the remission of sins" (Acts 2:38) to be forgiven by God. Be sure to ask yourself, "Who is this talking about?"

(6) **Recognize figurative language when you see it.** Jesus said, "I am the door" (Jn. 10:9). Does that mean He was a piece of wood with a knob and hinges?

No. It simply means that He is the entrance to eternal life. Herod was called a "fox" (Lk. 13:32). Does that mean he had four legs and whiskers? No. He was called a fox because he was cunning and sly. In warning against Judaizers, Paul said, "Beware of dogs" (Phil. 3:2), Peter likened the devil to a "roaring lion" (1 Pet. 5:8), and John called an immoral woman "Jezebel" (Rev. 2:20). Obviously "dogs," "lion," and "Jezebel" are not to be taken literally. These are figures of speech. Employ common sense and recognize figurative language when you see it.

(7) **Approach the scriptures with an honest heart.** Take an objective approach to your study, determined to put off all prejudices and preconceived ideas. It is possible to twist the scriptures unto your own destruction (2 Pet. 3:16). If it says it, believe it!

(8) **Remember that silence forbids.** We all recognize that silence forbids in the secular realm. The same is true in the religious realm as well. We must speak where the Bible speaks and be silent where the Bible is silent (1 Pet. 4:11). God does not want us to go beyond what is written. For instance, the old law was silent about priests coming from the tribe of Judah. Therefore, the law had to be changed in order for Jesus to be our high priest (Heb. 7:11-14). That is a classic example of silence forbidding an act. *Silence prohibits!*

Questions on Lesson 12

1. Why is Bible study important?

2. Does God expect us to understand His word? Explain.

3. Explain the difference between the old and new covenants.

4. What does it mean to keep a passage in context?

5. Why is it important to notice to whom commands were given?

6. Explain why honesty is important in studying the scriptures.

7. Is silence permissive or prohibitive? Explain.

Conclusion

I hope this book has encouraged you to "do all in the name of the Lord" (Col. 3:17). It is very easy to be led away from the divine pattern of the New Testament if we are not careful. Many counterfeit churches and misleading men have changed the plan of salvation and distorted the work, worship, and organization of the church. However, God has given mankind His perfect book to guide us in the paths of righteousness. Let us hold fast to the Word of God. — *Aaron*

www.ErhardtPublications.com

96 | The Simple Truth

Made in the USA
Charleston, SC
05 March 2015